FREEDOM from GOVERNMENT

DON'T TREAD ON ME

STATIST DELUSIONS

By Trent Goodbaudy

Trent Goodbaudy

Copyright © 2013 Trent Goodbaudy

All rights reserved. No portion of this book may be reproduced, stored in a retrieval system, or transmitted in any form or by any means-electronic, mechanical, photocopy, recording, scanning, or other-except for brief quotations in critical reviews or articles, without the prior permission of the author.

Published in Portland, Oregon by PDXdzyn. PDXdzyn is a trademark of Trent Goodbaudy. PDXdzyn titles may be purchased in bulk for educational, business, fund-raising, or sales promotional use. For information, please send email to info@pdxdzyn.com.

Also visit http://freedomfromgovernment.org

Printed in the United States of America.

ISBN-13: **978-1482027549**
ISBN-10: **1482027542**

DEDICATION

This book is dedicated to people that want to be free and do the right thing.

CONTENTS

	Introduction	3 – 6
1	"Violence And The Use Of Force Is Necessary."	7 – 24
2	"Government Has A Divine Right To Rule Over Us."	25 – 36
3	"It's Our Fault Because We Voted For This Guy."	37 – 47
4	"Monopolies Would Abound Without Government."	49 – 52
5	"You Have A Social Contract, That's Why."	53 – 64
6	"We Deserve Government Healthcare."	65 – 78
7	"The Economy Would Collapse Without Government."	79 – 88
8	"Sacrificing a Little Liberty For Security Never Hurt Anyone."	89 - 99
9	"Taxes Are Fees For Services."	101 – 122
10	"Government Is Necessary For Infrastructure, Police, Courts."	123 - 129
11	"Take A Benefit From The Government, And You Endorse It."	131 – 133
12	"Why Don't You Go Live Somewhere Else, Like Somalia."	135 – 138
13	"Without Rules, There Would Be Chaos."	139 – 147
	Conclusion	149 – 152
	About The Author	159

ACKNOWLEDGMENTS

Some of the people that I have been influenced by:
Mark Passio, Marc Stevens, Robert Menard, Dean Clifford, Stefan Molyneux, Santos Bonacci, Michael Shanklin, Aaron Hawkins, Jared Dalen, Harold Austerman, Michael Yung Jai, Rob Halford, Dave Bleicher, Craig Brockie, Brendan McCormick, Dean Kory, Donald Hamm, Chris Fleming, Cody Carllson, Michael Rethati, Mike Carparelli, Jonny Otf Thrombosis, Peter Schiff, Judge Andrew Napolitano, Ron Paul, John Harris, Adam Kokesh, Pastor Steven Anderson, Lysander Spooner, Noam Chomsky, Tami Pepperman, William Cooper, Phil Schneider, Scott Duncan, and I know that there are likely more that I am forgetting ...
please forgive me for not mentioning you as well.

INTRODUCTION

I suppose that since I have included the word "statist" in the title of this book, before I proceed I should briefly explain what it is about. In case you are not aware of what a statist is, I will explain exactly what I believe a statist to be, and what I am trying to achieve by writing this book.

"Statist" as defined by Merriam-Webster.com is **": an advocate of statism"**. So, perhaps the definition of "Statism" would be appropriate at this point; "Statism" as defined by Merriam-Webster.com is **": concentration of economic controls and planning in the hands of a highly centralized government often extending to government ownership of industry"**

That was a rather dry and uninteresting yet accurate definition, but maybe I should share what a statist is to *me*, in easy-to-understand, common terms.

In my mind; a statist has an unending, all enduring faith and whole-hearted support of their government and its practice of forcing compliance with its legislation through violence. A statist believes that government is necessary for society, and if you do not support your government it does not matter because you will be forced into compliance. There is no opting out of your servitude, there is only compliance. Comparable in ways, to hardcore theism, someone that is a statist often times believes that government is not only necessary, but should be involved in making decisions for people, to the extent that violence and coercion is used. The majority of statists are typically, literally stuck in the left-right paradigm of two-party politics.

Have you thought about your true political affiliation? Most of us believe that there are only two main choices; either Democrat or Republican. When in reality there are many more political systems. From collectivism to socialism, anarchism to state-capitalism, fascism to communism, most of which are largely misunderstood by the general public. For example, did you know that The People's Republic of China operates under a State-Capitalism political system; and not one of Communism as the majority of Americans believe? I don't want to get too much into explaining what the many other political system models are and how they operate (as this would be a book in itself). Although I do want to build an awareness of what statism is, and introduce you to less archaic and viable alternatives to it. I believe that the information, when presented properly speaks for itself in terms of practicality and ethical alternatives to our current system.

Currently, our societies understanding of its need for government is based on the principal that we are unable to be responsible for ourselves, and as a solution, we have granted the government a divine right to rule over us, and the right to use force and coercion against us to get us to comply. Don't believe me? Try not paying your taxes or driving your vehicle without registering it with the government and see how long it takes to be forced or coerced into compliance. So many other species live on this planet in relative harmony, but our species, the Human Race is compelled to imprison ourselves in a box made of government and as a result we severely limit our abilities as sentient beings with God-given rights, not government granted privileges. This type of society, essentially a security and control matrix, also inadvertently introduces a plethora of psychological issues including depression, hopelessness, anxiety, psychopathy, and many other conditions up to and including, suicide and homicide.

From birth we are indoctrinated to believe that we have masters. A great majority of Americans believe that the government exists to tell others what to do. They believe that people need to be "helped" into making the right choices by forcing them to do what the state feels is best for them in the form of legislation through law enforcement and corrections. What is wrong with letting people make their own decisions about every aspect of their own life? Except, of course for when infringing on the free will of others or doing harm to others, why shouldn't we have the liberty to do as we please during our lifetime? Why do we need to have a government that threatens us with violence and coercion that we *must* support it or violence and force will be used against us? I think it is time to start thinking about alternatives.

We only have one life. We have one chance. We each have maybe around one hundred years if we are lucky, to complete a fulfilling life here on planet Earth. Why do we need to grant the powers of master over us to a faceless corporate entity with no soul, and no motivation to protect us? This book is about the most common arguments I have heard people use that support statism, and why they are obsolete, oppressive, or even *delusional*, and what we can do to improve conditions on this planet for all of humanity.

1 "THE USE OF FORCE IS NECESSARY."

First, I must declare that while looking at all of the heinous things police officers and other agents of government are capable of, it's important to remember that we are all equal as human beings, and most police are wonderful human beings that are just as capable of love and compassion as anyone else. Many of them choose their profession for noble reasons. They want to provide for the public safety, help people, and fight for justice. At the end of the day we must remember that police are people, just like you and me. The difference is that they have a badge, and the sanction to execute government policy by force. Because of this, it is important to make sure that the protocols of government are just and that the individuals holding the badges treat citizens fairly. This is our responsibility, not as Americans or even as individuals but simply as members of communities that want people to be treated fairly, and want justice to be done.

If you are a statist, chances are that you have never heard of the non-aggression principle (also referred to as the non-aggression axiom). Most libertarians base their views about morality and the role of government around the non-aggression principle.

The non-aggression principle is the idea that no matter how disgusting, immoral, or improper you believe an act to be, you have no right to use *force* to stop someone from committing that act, *unless* that act itself involves the initiation of force against another person (or person's property).

The principle is simple and straight forward; it is wrong to initiate force against another person or group of people. This is by no means a passive or pacifist doctrine; it is absolutely permissible to use force in response to force, in order to protect or defend one's person or property, to enforce a contract, or punish someone for failure to adhere to the terms of a contract.

However, it is not permissible to use force to attack your neighbor, steal another person's property, or stop someone from using their justly acquired property in a manner that does not aggress upon another individual.

By applying the non-aggression principle to all aspects of life, a just and coherent philosophy of non-interventionism becomes clear: if no one is being harmed besides those people voluntarily engaged in the act, leave it alone. It is that simple. You don't have to like or respect or engage in prostitution, homosexual relations, religion, or the use of drugs, alcohol, tobacco, etc, but you do *not* have the right to stop any adult from engaging in any of these acts.

The non-aggression principle is a very important part of the natural rights philosophy.

Every person is the owner of their own body and has the right to do with their body as they see fit. People can also acquire property by using one of three different methods: homesteading, voluntary exchange, and theft. Homesteading involves taking unowned resources and improving them, while voluntary exchange involves the unforced transfer of resources from a person (or persons) to another person (or persons). Both of these two methods are fully consistent with the non-aggression principle—by definition, neither homesteading or voluntary exchange involves the initiation of force.

When the non-aggression principle is violated, property is acquired in the third method: theft. Physical acts of violence or threats of violence against others are violations of a person's right to self-ownership.

Even if one rejects the doctrine of natural rights in favor of a utilitarian (ie, the common good) view, the non-aggression principle is still important.

Man is a social animal. For the most part, we seek to engage in activities which promote the social benefit. Activities which violate the non-aggression principle tend to disrupt the peace by inviting violent retaliation. For example, if I kill or harm a member of your family (or attempt to do so), you are likely to respond by seeking revenge on me. These types of feuds can spiral out of control and disrupt the peaceful cooperation on which society depends. The best way to keep the peace that is essential to the existence of society, is to adhere to the non-aggression principle.

Thus, whether you subscribe to natural rights theories or whether you support some sort of utilitarian view, it is in the best interests of both individuals and society that people adhere to the non-aggression principle.

As we have seen, violations of the non-aggression principle which are committed by individuals can disrupt the peace. However, violations of the non-aggression principle committed by the government are infinitely more egregious. This is because the government grants itself the power to do things that no individual could ever be permitted to do.

Only the government (or those under the protection of the government) can confiscate money from people without their permission and give it to other people and call it "public policy." Government redistribution of wealth and granting of special privileges is aggression because it prevents people from using their own property in a peaceful manner of their choosing.

Only the government can commit mass murder against civilians and call it a "defensive war." A bombing campaign in a densely populated civilian area which results in civilian deaths is murder; it doesn't matter if the bombing was done by a rogue terrorist or by an Air Force member acting under order from the President. Murder is murder. It doesn't matter who does it.

Since I mentioned murder; what is the difference between murder and killing anyway? Do you know? Murder is the use of violence, and killing is the use of force. Murder is offensive, killing is defensive. There is never a just cause for murder; it is the initiation of violence. If someone broke into your home and you killed them, it would not be considered murder because you were using force in a defensive capacity. You were presumably justified in killing them because your rights were being violated when they violated your private property.

When it comes to using force and coercion on people, the government is king. Only the government can throw human beings in cages for the "crime" of recreationally smoking a plant in their own home. Smoking marijuana on your couch does not violate the non-aggression principle; raiding someone's house and confiscating their marijuana does.

It is essentially impossible for government to act without violating the non-aggression principle. This is because mandatory taxation is coercion, theft, and extortion. All of these acts violate the non-aggression principle. Taking people's money without their permission is theft. Any business regulation, permit requirement, governmental zoning restriction, anti-drug law, restriction of consensual acts deemed to be "immoral," etc. are violations of the non-aggression principle because they prevent people from using their justly acquired resources in a peaceful manner of their choosing.

Every government act involves a violation of the non-aggression principle. For, even when government is acting to stop one person from aggressing against another, it is doing so using resources that have been obtained via theft. When *you* violate the non-aggression principle, your actions may be devastating and cause harm, but they are limited by the amount of damage that one person can cause with whatever resources that are available for them to use. However, when the government violates the non-aggression principle, it does so with other people's money subject only to how much damage it can inflict before enough people get angry enough to either withdraw support or threaten revolution. It also does so under the guise of legality. But intelligent people know that an unjust law is no law at all.

Thus, the only way for government to act without aggressing on the rights of its citizens by violating the non-aggression principle would be for the government to set the exact policies that each individual would choose on their own and rely on truly voluntary donations to do so. In other words, the government's best option is to do nothing at all.

In the words of the French economist, Anne-Robert-Jacques Turgot:

"The policy to pursue, therefore, is to follow the course of nature, without pretending to direct it. For, in order to direct trade and commerce it would be necessary to be able to have knowledge of all of the variations of needs, interests, and human industry in such detail as is physically impossible to obtain even by the most able, active, and circumstantial government. And even if a government did possess such a multitude of detailed knowledge, the result would be to let things go precisely as they do of themselves, by the sole action of the interests of men prompted by free competition."

This isn't just the stuff of libertarian philosophers. The rapper Lil' Jon famously uttered the phrase *"Don't start no shit, there won't be no shit!"*

This concept is remarkably simple: do not initiate the use of force against another person. Respect their right to engage in peaceful activities on their own property in any manner that they see fit.

The use of force should be the final option ever chosen, but it must remain an option.

The use of force is only necessary and justified as an act of defense, or as a last resort to defend a friend or family member from an impending or imminent attack. This can be extended to defending property or homeland from violence or an attack with force as well. If we truly live in a free society, we should not be forced to do things that we do not want to do. And forcing people to do things that they don't want to do, seems to be what the government has been doing. Why do we continue to allow this to happen?

When you think of what your rights are in particular, simply think in terms of "right" and "wrong". If it is MORALLY right... you have the right to do it. That is where the term "rights" came from... right and wrong. If we are morally doing right, we have the right to do it... we are within our rights. Get it? So many do not understand that morality or common sense is a law that is above us; everyone "stands under" this law because it is based on morals there is no one above common sense.

Simply stated, government exists to exercise authority over people's lives, it is a ruler, a master, an owner of people. The problem is that we allow the government to exercise authority over people's lives, even though it has no soul, no compassion, and not even a duty to protect us anymore (refer to DeShaney v. Winnebago County, United stated Supreme court, 1989). Knowing this, how could we continue to allow it to exercise authority over people in a coercive manor? We should not be so scared of our natural state of being, or Natural Law. When I say Natural law I am referring to the law that is above us, the law of right and wrong, the law that no man is above, the law that we all stand under inherently. An example of natural law states that if someone is violating our rights through violence, we have the inherent right to respond with the use of force.

The government is authorized to use force, but it is not authorized to use violence and coercion. How can we give the government a right that we do not have as individuals? When the government justifies these wrong actions, it is trying to create a right that doesn't exist. So what the government is doing when it uses violence and coercion on people is actually delegating a right that it does not have. It is not ok to condone violence; no one has a right to use violence.

When I use the term 'violence', it is different than the term 'force'; the difference is that violence is initiating the use of force or coercion on an individual who has not violated anyone's rights. Force can only be used in defense of an individual whose rights have been violated, where violence is initiating force on someone unnecessarily. Force is looked at as a use, while violence is looked at as abuse. To determine who is using violence, we must determine who initiated the conflict. Who started it? If force is used without right, it is coercive and non-moral. There is no such thing as a proper and moral use of violence, and the proper use of force means that it was morally used.

How many times have we heard a government agent using violence say; "I'm just doing my job!"? I personally have heard it many times. To me this says that the government agent's personal collection of money and resources usurps someone's free will. This is absurd and also reminiscent of how a psychopath will justify their actions with irrational claims. Psychopaths will often rationalize their behavior, blame others, and deny people their inherent rights. If someone or something does not have a right, a wrong cannot be delegated in its place.

A human being cannot delegate a right to another human being that the first human being does not have. Two human beings cannot delegate a right to a third human being that the other two human beings do not have. This makes me wonder where Congress got their rights to do anything?

Freedom *from* Government: Statist Delusions

To restore our freedom, we need to live by the non-aggression axiom and revert back to Natural law, where there are no rulers, and no masters. People currently rely on their servitude to the extent that they feel that they would be lost or confused without a ruler or master, but that is just a fear instilled in us by means of our servitude. A slave on a plantation would be utterly frightened of the big world beyond the plantation boundary and not having his master to care for him, yet we all know that he can do so much better on his own, being allowed to own property and to keep the fruits of his labor. Going back to natural law will not cause chaos, nor will it be mayhem in the streets, how can we even know what it would be like... we have never experienced it. We are damaged animals, our spirit has been broken, we are domesticated, and we are slaves. We are stuck in an illusory construct that only exists in a diseased psyche. There really are no rulers and no masters anyway; just claims of authority, and acceptance of these claims by the brainwashed. There really is no government other than what you choose to be governed by; they only have the authority that you grant them.

During the American Revolutionary war, our forefathers were looked at as terrorists by the crown. What made them terrorists? Were they labeled terrorists due to the fact that they wanted to be free? The early American colonies use of force was vindicated because the violence was initiated by the crown. Back then there were no airplanes, these agents of government were so dedicated that they spent weeks on a boat risking scurvy and other ill fates to come over and coerce people they had likely never even met before.

The use of force when no one's rights have been violated equals violence, plain and simple. People should not be given the authority to use violence on another in the form of a shiny metal. None of us have the right to use violence to attain our goals; therefore it is not a right we can delegate to a third party either. It is not a right that any of us have, so how could the government (who gets all of its power from the people) have that right? It isn't ok for me to make a bunch of rules with penalties and then go out and enforce them through violence, so there should be no violent "enforcement" by other entities either. Especially not by corporate entities that are biased to the bottom line and rarely held accountable, or often times delegated powers are used by its agents to empower their own ego. If someone knows that they can use violence and they then will be exonerated, they are more likely to justify the use of violence individually, especially if they suffer psychological issues.

Our society has been taken over by psychopaths. Psychopathy is a personality disorder that has been variously characterized by shallow emotions (including reduced fear, a lack of empathy, and stress tolerance), cold-heartedness, egocentricity, superficial charm, manipulativeness, irresponsibility, impulsivity, criminality, antisocial behavior, a lack of remorse, and a parasitic lifestyle. Government psychopaths believe that *you* don't have the right to use coercive force on people, but they do. There is also a kind of learned psychopathy that exists in our culture, and these secondary psychopaths are not intentionally psychopaths. They have assumed their condition because they are just so focused on their own survival that they have compromised their own morals.

Is it morally wrong to initiate force against people that have not violated anyone's rights? Should the government take action against people that have not violated anybody's rights? For example; most people are peaceful and just go to work every morning and work for an honest living, is it right for the government to take action against people that have not done anything wrong? Would taxing the school teacher in order to give money to the farmer be considered taking an action against the teacher? When the government is in the business of redistributing wealth among its people, it amounts to nothing more than legalized theft. I believe in respecting other people's judgment, and offering a value. If people see a value in something than they will not need to be forced to pay for someone else. A normal person would not think that they can just go around and take things from other people without value for consideration and without consent. We call that stealing. How could it ever be morally proper for the government to force the people that it derives its power from to pay for something that they do not choose to pay for? This is how redistribution of wealth is the initiation of force against people that have not violated anyone else's rights, and amounts to nothing more than legalized theft. If we do not support something, we should not be forced to pay for it.

The Declaration of Independence states that all legitimate governmental power is derived from the people, and that the government actually gets its power from the "consent of the governed", and that the sole purpose of governments is to secure unalienable rights that we are "endowed by our creator" with. Not privileges granted by government. The Declaration also states; "That whenever any Form of Government becomes destructive of these ends [protecting rights], it is the Right of the People to alter or to abolish it, and to institute new Government, laying its foundation on such principles and organizing its powers in such form, as to them shall seem most likely to effect their Safety and Happiness. Prudence, indeed, will dictate that

Governments long established should not be changed for light and transient causes; and accordingly all experience hath shewn, that mankind are more disposed to suffer, while evils are sufferable, than to right themselves by abolishing the forms to which they are accustomed. But when a long train of abuses and usurpations, pursuing invariably the same Object evinces a design to reduce them under absolute Despotism, it is their right, it is their duty, to throw off such Government, and to provide new Guards for their future security."

So we must truly ask ourselves, exactly where does the power of government come from? Does it come from the citizens? Or does it come from the barrel of a gun? We as individual citizens don't even have the right to initiate physical force against other citizens that haven't violated anybody's rights, so that definitely could not be a power that we have given government, as it is not ours to even give. There is no way that we could have delegated the right to use force against people who have not violated anyone else's rights, as the people do not even retain such a right.

The use of force may be acceptable when such a situation justifies it (such as when someone's rights or property have been violated or in a self-defense situation), but you can't force someone to make a choice or the choice is no longer theirs. A choice that is made for you is an order, not a moral decision. A decision realized through the use of force fundamentally can never be considered right. A choice that you are forced to make can be considered necessary or justified, however justification is subjective and can be manufactured and mean different things to different people. Anything can be justified, justification by nature is relative.

The government is violence. It does not ask you nicely to obey the law, it arrests and convicts you. So the question is basically the same as "is government necessary?" I do believe that law enforcement does have a place, but only if someone has had either their rights or property violated. As a moral society, we should not condone violence by any party.

Force is absolutely necessary to protect a man's home and family. This does not mean one should seek confrontation but if the safety of one's spouse or family is threatened, being willing to engage in a forceful act may be the only way to protect them. This principle could be extrapolated to the country as a whole to say that the use of force is necessary in the event of invasion to combat invaders. Take for example the story of the American heroes on 9/11 that attacked the terrorists on the plane over Pennsylvania, forcing the plane down and saving countless lives. In events like these where one's family and home are threatened, defensive force is sometimes the only solution.

Violence however is becoming far too normalized in America, violence is portrayed as fun, and the top grossing video game last year was a first-person army shooter. We are being conditioned, desensitized, and this is because people are taught through violence on TV and wars that violence is not only necessary, but somehow entertaining. This can end up manifesting itself in devastating cases of domestic violence, which often repeats itself in cycles. There is no moral reason to use violence.

In this country, we accept the notion that violence or the use of force by coercion against those that have violated no right is somehow necessary, and we recognize it in our judicial system. We allow, as a country, an individual to be jailed for not paying taxes. We do not view this as "immoral", and many feel that this is acceptable.

Where do we draw the line between violence and other forms of coercion though? Slavery isn't always necessarily violent, that is until the slave tries to leave, or sell the products of their labor themselves. Equally bosses and the state aren't necessarily violent until we disobey them. So often revolutionaries are seen as 'starting it' because they draw out the unspoken everyday violence needed to make state capitalism work, when in fact the violence is already there as concealed 'constituted power' as opposed to our creative-destructive 'constituting power'. Slavery is inherently violent as becoming a slave means coercive dispossession of the body (slaves usually don't just volunteer to be slaves).

Unfortunately, if we cannot stop the usurpations of the people's power by government, violence will continue to be deemed necessary, and unfortunately they have many guns, bullets, and other compliance inducing devices. So while knowing that defensive force may be necessary at some point, it is not preferred and a fight that we really want to avoid. The media will of course always spin any violent action to exonerate the government. The portrayal of violence is carefully manipulated by the media.

We need to modify our perception of violence. Authority creates a monopoly over the definition and legitimacy of "violence". There can never be a definitive description of violence that can rigidly characterize one act as being violent or not as long as the government and media are defining these terms. The presuppositions of our society along with the mainstream media influence are keeping people in the dark.

> *To be governed is to be watched, inspected, spied upon, directed, law-driven, numbered, regulated,*

> *enrolled, indoctrinated, preached at, controlled, checked, estimated, valued, censured, and commanded, by creatures who have neither the right nor the wisdom nor the virtue to do so. To be governed is to be at every operation, at every transaction noted, registered, counted, taxed, stamped, measured, numbered, assessed, licensed, authorized, admonished, prevented, forbidden, reformed, corrected, and punished. It is, under pretext of public utility, and in the name of the general interest, to be placed under contribution, drilled, fleeced, exploited, monopolized, extorted from, squeezed, hoaxed, robbed; then, at the slightest resistance, the first word of complaint, to be repressed, fined, vilified, harassed, hunted down, abused, clubbed, disarmed, bound, choked, imprisoned, judged, condemned, shot, deported, sacrificed, sold, betrayed; and to crown all, mocked, ridiculed, derided, outraged, and dishonored. -*
> **Pierre-Joseph Proudhon**

Violence often diminishes the power of those who employ it, necessitating the use of more violence in an attempt to gain or maintain control.

Power and violence are not the same. Power is psychological, a moral force that makes people want to obey. Violence enforces obedience through physical coercion. Those who use violence may manage to temporarily impose their will, but their command is always tenuous because when the violence ends, or the threat of it lessens, there is even less incentive to obey the authorities. Control through violence requires constant vigilance. Too little violence is ineffective; too much violence generates revolt.

Violence is the weapon of choice for the impotent. Those who don't have much power often attempt to control or influence others by using violence. Violence rarely creates power. On the contrary, groups or individuals that use violence often find their actions diminish what little power they *do* have.

Groups that oppose governments often try to compensate for their perceived lack of power by using violence. Such violence simply reinforces state power. A terrorist that blows up a building or assassinates a politician gives government the excuse it wants to crack down on individual liberties and expand its sphere of influence.

When a government turns to violence, it is because it feels its power is slipping away. Governments that rule through violence are weak. Dictators have always had to rely on terror against their own populations to compensate for their powerlessness.

The U.S. would feel no need to fight wars in Latin America or the Persian Gulf if it had power in those regions. The only way to maintain control in the absence of power is through the continual use of violence. Protracted violence results in diminished power, making more violence necessary.

The government would have you believe that you can't just TAKE your freedom, but in reality that is the ONLY way it can be done.

Freedom *from* Government: Statist Delusions

So once again, just in case you missed it:

The FORCE v. VIOLENCE dichotomy

-Force -
- The capacity to do work or cause physical change; energy, strength, active power.
- Action which is IN harmony with morality and Natural law, because it does not violate the rights of others.
- Action which one always possesses the right to take (including defending oneself against violence.

- Violence -

- The immoral use of physical power to coerce, compel, or restrain.
- Initiation of coercive action which is in opposition to morality and natural law because it involves the violation of others rights.
- Action which one never possesses the right to take.

You can't stop people from doing what they want to do. Banning products just leads to black markets, where entrepreneurs are replaced by criminals, eventually leading to brutal gang wars among other negative outcomes. The government spends trillions trying to prevent people from harming themselves, and all in vein.

A statist will have you believe that force is necessary under certain conditions, and while this may be true, there are no conditions in which violence is truly necessary.

We, as reasoning, thinking, inhabitants of this planet, always have other choices. Violence of any kind is not necessary for the benefit, furtherance, or preservation of the human race. We have other choices. We have language. We can communicate. We can defuse a violent situation, or avoid it. We do not have to take out our frustrations, wishes for gratification, resources, food...domination...anything that drives us, in the form of violence.

We have BRAINS! We can figure out another way, a better way, to resolve any dispute, than war.

We do not need violence. We don't need to hurt and maim and kill each other. We don't need to do this. We don't need to stockpile nuclear weapons. We don't need to gather arms which could devastate and depopulate of any life a whole continent, or the whole world.

We know we don't need it. We know we don't need violence.

2 "GOVERNMENT HAS A DIVINE RIGHT TO RULE OVER US."

Why government? Where did it come from? Why does mankind seem to love creating institutions to enslave itself? History is a great teacher. It often provides clues that enable us to understand the present and future.

There are four main "theories" that attempt to legitimize government and explain its origins, and although they are called "theories" they are by no means scientifically understood and cannot be proven. They are more like educated guesses, but no one really knows for sure. The four theories are; the Force theory, the Evolution or Incremental theory, the Social Contract theory, and the Divine Right theory.

The **Force theory**, (also known as the *force theory of state*) holds that the state was born as a result of force, in other words; aggression, war, conquest and subjugation. The Force theory holds that governments were first organized when one person or a group of persons conquered a given territory, and then forced everyone living within that territory to submit to their will. In ancient times a strong man with the help of his supporters dominated the weaker people of his tribe and established the political relation of command and obedience. This was the beginning of the state. Later on, a strong tribe dominated the weaker ones and in this way a kingdom came into being. With the passage of time a strong king subjugated the weaker ones and created an empire. Institutions were created to make people work and to collect all or part of what they produced for their masters/conquerors. Keep in mind that prior to the last 100 or even fewer years, open slavery was widely accepted throughout the world, and not seen as wrong.

The force theory suggests that the first governments were essentially coercive, that they were instruments for asserting the authority of one person, or one group of people, over an entire society.

The Force theory of state gives more importance to the role of force. Force is not the only element, which creates the state, and preserves it. Today the supporters of this theory forget that force is like a highly-addictive narcotic drug, and positions authorized to use liberal force attract and create psychopaths. Also, history has proven that those who come to power by force are also overthrown by force.

The supporters of the force theory of government forget one basic point that "It is not *force* but *will* which is the basis of the state." Force can be used, but without the consent of the people it is likely to fail. Any state that fails to learn this lesson of history becomes non-existent. The force theory is not a good idea for a government for people who wish to have freedom. A dictator or a group of dictators would make all decisions and there would be no rights for its citizens. The people would have no say and would not be able to vote on anything. The dictator would have supreme control.

The **Evolution** or **Incremental theory** states that primitive families formed the population long ago, and it was the heads of these families that became the government. This theory holds that government developed gradually, step-by-step, in small increments, beginning with the family. A family would settle a particular territory and claim it as its own, and as a result the territory would become a sovereign state. The primitive family, in most cases with the husband or the father as the head, united with other families, often relatives, for mutual protection and to work cooperatively to survive.

Someone, often one of the older males, became the leader, in order to make decision-making easier and to settle disputes. As the years went by, the number of families involved grew larger and the "government" progressively became larger and more formalized.

The incremental theory suggests that first governments were voluntary. The people willingly formed governments of a cooperative nature in order to be social, to defend themselves and to work together for common purposes. This suggestion is very optimistic in its conclusion, but history shows that states were typically not set up voluntarily. The earliest governments were not much more than a ruling class of slave hunters who understood that because people could produce more than they consumed, they were worth hunting, capturing, domesticating or breaking in, and owning.

The earliest Chinese and Egyptian empires were in reality human farms where people were hunted, captured, and domesticated like any other form of livestock. The ruling class kept the majority of their subject's productivity, in return for food and shelter if they were lucky. Throughout history, and through our not so distant past mankind has been used as a means of support for its masters.

The **Social Contract theory** holds that a population in a given territory agrees to contract some of their inherent power to government as needed to promote the well-being of all. People lived poorly and to improve their lives people could enter into a social contract where a superior person would rule over the rest. I have dedicated a chapter to the social contract later in the book, but for now I would like to dedicate the reminder of this chapter to the Divine Right theory of government.

The **Divine Right theory** states that God either created the state, or God endowed the king to rule over the people within the state. This theory relies on a solid religious presence that agrees with the state to be perpetuated; this theory also easily justifies the use of violence and coercive force as divine ordinance. The government is made up of those who are chosen by God to rule a specific territory. The population must obey its ruler, or face the wrath of God. In the case of ancient Egypt, people listened and obeyed – at least, as much as they did – because Pharaoh was, in theory, a god as well as the king.

The Divine Right was a theory of government that was effective in controlling the population, but is now obsolete. And there was really only one main principle to the government's authority. You had to believe in God. You had to believe that He gave out job assignments. You also had to believe that He didn't mind when

His employees and agents made a mess of things ... or even when they contradicted his own orders. With a firm belief in religion though, the authority of the government could not be denied. Looking at the history of the monarchs who were thought to have been given this divine authority, you would have to conclude that God was either a very tolerant task-master, or a very negligent one. Adultery, murder, thieving, lying – there was hardly one of God's commandments they obeyed.

As a theory of government, the divine right theory might have been okay had it not been for the kings themselves. Some were reasonable men. Others were tyrants. Many were incompetent, largely irrelevant and silly. Upon comparison, it was very difficult to believe that they had all been selected by God, without also believing that God was just choosing His most important managers at random. Kings were not especially smart. Not especially bold or especially timid. Not especially wise or stupid. For all intents and purposes, they were just like everyone else. Sometimes smart. Sometimes dumb. Sometimes good. Sometimes evil. And always subject to influence.

Towards the end of the 18th century, the divine right theory lost its following. The Church, the monarch and the feudal system all seemed to lose market share. The Enlightenment had made people begin to wonder. Then, the beginning of the "Industrial Revolution" made them stir.

Divine right was based on a metaphysical assertion. Despite "ultimate authority," kings engaged "intellectuals" to provide supporting propaganda for the claim. Their efforts worked for a long time. As late as 1729, Thomas Paine saw fit to speak about the lingering right of heredity:

"[T]he idea of hereditary legislators is as inconsistent as that of hereditary judges, or hereditary juries; and as absurd as an hereditary mathematician, or an hereditary wise man; and as ridiculous as an hereditary poet laureate."

The interesting parallel to today is the ancient regimes' use of "intellectuals" as court propagandists. The same model exists today. The propagandists who led our country to its current dismal state, it seems to me, are economists. Today's metaphysicians are called economic advisors.

The "government that governs best," as Jefferson put it, "is the one that governs least." This is, of course, another way of saying that government – like every other natural phenomenon – is subject to the law of declining marginal utility. A little government could be a good thing, but too big a government has never proven effective and beneficial for the individual. The energy put into a system of public order, dispute resolution, and certain minimal public services may give a positive return on investment. But the point of diminishing returns is reached quickly.

Government – according the Liberal philosophers of the 18th and 19th century – was supposed to get out of the way so that the 'invisible hand' would guide men to productive, fruitful lives. Many have falsely been led to believe that the arm attached to the invisible hand was the arm of God. Others believed that not even God was necessary. Men, without central planning or God to guide them, would create a 'spontaneous order', which would be a lot nicer than the one created by kings, dictators or popular assemblies.

The divine right to rule is one of the most important doctrines in history yet most people don't understand this concept. The first step in understanding the concept of the divine right to rule is to know its history. Once you understand the history of the concept you are ready to learn what the actual concept is and how it works in government. Despite the fact that in most countries the belief in and practice of the divine right to rule has long retired, there were and still are many strengths of the concept. Of course, where there are strengths, there will always be some weaknesses and examples where this concept did not work. Understanding the concept of the divine right to rule will allow you to comprehend the origin of past and present forms of government all over the world.

The divine right to rule has a long and diverse history that has touched almost every civilization known. The divine right to rule is not a modern concept. In fact, it is so ancient that scholars find it hard to pinpoint the exact place or culture that first used the concept to rule. However, historians do know three main cultures that practiced the concept in very early history.

The Egyptian culture was one of the first to follow the idea of divine right. The Egyptians had rulers called Pharaohs who were believed to be the earthly incarnation of the Egyptian sun god, Ra. Therefore, god technically chose the ruler of the Egyptian people. This belief meant that if an Egyptian were to disobey his Pharaoh, than he was actually disobeying his god. To question the authority of a Pharaoh and suggest that they were not the desired ruler was to tell god that his ruling was undesirable. In Egypt the concept was first adopted to create a "world empire" and amass great recourses and protection with witch to continue the Egyptian conquest. Another civilization that believed in the divine right to rule was Ancient China. Ancient China called this concept "the mandate of heaven." Unlike the ancient Egyptians, the Ancient

Chinese did not believe in an earthly incarnation of their god. They thought that the heavens gave a dynasty its approval to rule.

In the case of Rome – with the exception of Caligula's claims – and the Mongol empires, the theory was similarly simple, though different. Tamerlane made no claim to divinity. He merely made it clear what he would do to you if you resisted him. Towns that submitted were generally governed passably, according to the standards of the day... and taxed, but not razed to the ground. Those that contested his authority were destroyed, often with all the inhabitants killed.

In Rome and out on the steppes, those who controlled the 'government' were in the favored position. They could reach out and impose their will on those who were not favored; which is exactly what they did. As long as they were able, the insiders took from the outsiders. In both cases, the outsiders were literally outside the ruling group and its homeland.

This is perhaps a good place to point out that government is a phenomenon, not a system. Like a host's relationship to a cancer, government relies upon an already functioning society to be given power, and a government's power is always derived from its participants. The down side is that this power is usually used against those the government is supposed to be serving. It is best understood as a fight between the outsiders and the insiders. The insiders always control the government ... and use it to conquer and control the outsiders. Why do they want to do so? The usual reasons, of course ... wealth, status, and power.

None can deny the appeal of wealth, power, and status, except for maybe either a feebleminded individual or a saint. And usually the easiest, fastest way to get it is to take it away from someone else. So this has now evolved to the government's role, and some people still even believe that it has a divine right to do so. Today only government can take something away from someone else lawfully. Why? Simple, because the governments make the laws, and we follow them.

So a small group of Romans were able to reach beyond their home town, for nearly 1,000 years, taking wealth from people on the outside. One tribe fell under their control, then another; one town, then on to another, and another. With the power, prestige, and wealth always flowing back home to Rome.

The Roman Empire's demise was eventually due to problems with the insiders. Rome itself was divided. During the Republican period, the insiders were the leading families who controlled the Senate. Then would come the dictators, the emperors, and the rogues who were able to eventually get control of the government.

Often, they were military men, popular or cunning generals who rose through the ranks, murdered their rivals, and took the reins of power for themselves. Each brought in new insiders ... and kicked out some of the old ones. Rome sizzled with intrigue ... and sometimes erupted into open warfare, with one group of insiders battling it out with another.

After Rome fell, barbarian tribes swept over Europe. Local strongmen were able to set up their own governments. There was little theory or justification involved. They used brute force to take what they wanted. Then they settled down to govern. One local lord provided protection from other local lords. All demanded payment, tribute, wealth and power. In the largely un-moneyed economies of the Dark Ages, taxes were made in the form of a share of output ... or a number of his days of labor. A serf typically worked one day in ten for his lord and master.

The local warlord and his entourage were the insiders. They took from the outsiders as much as they could get away with; or as much as they thought it prudent to demand. Some even asserted a *droit du seigneur*: a putative legal right allowing the lord of a medieval estate to take the virginity of his serfs' maiden daughters. Known in France by the more carnal expression "the right to the thigh"; the local chief demanded the right to deflower the brides of his peasants. Even as recently as the beginning of the last century, Kurdish chieftains claimed the right to bed Armenian brides on their wedding night.

As the Dark Ages progressed, government became less locally peculiar. Across Europe, serfs, lords, and vassals knit themselves together into the feudal system. One governed a small area and was in turn governed by another, who governed a bigger one. At the top was the king, who owed his allegiance to God himself.

Justifying and explaining the phenomenon of government also evolved. How to make sense of it? Why was one man powerful and rich and another weak and poor? Europe was Christianized by then. All men were supposed to be equal in God's eyes. How come they were so different in the eyes of each other?

Reaching back into antiquity, the doctrine of the "Divine Right of Kings" was developed to explain it. Scholars did not maintain that kings were divine, because that would undermine the foundations of Judeo-Christian monotheism. Instead, they claimed that kings had a special role to play, that they were appointed ... and anointed, by God (through his ministers in the church of St. Peter), to rule. Some people thought the kings were descended directly from the line of Jesus Christ. Others thought that God gave kings a "divine" right to govern in His name.

In the fixed order of the world, each person had a job to do. One was a woodward. Another tended to livestock. Another was a bringer of water. A third was a king. Each man did his duty.

Scholars in the middle ages spent a lot of time on the issue. As a theory of government it seemed coherent and logical. But there were traps and dead ends in it. If the right to rule were given by God, man could not contradict Him. But men did. One divinely-appointed ruler met another divinely-appointed ruler on the field of battle. Only one could win. What kind of game was God playing?

And if God granted a man the right to rule other men, did that mean that every order he gave must be obeyed, just as though it had come from the mouth of God himself? And what if the king seemed not to be doing God's work at all? Adultery was clearly a no-no. God disapproved of it. But kings often made it a habit and a sport. Did not the king defile his body and betray his Lord? In an effort to explain away the problem, scholars put forth the idea that the king actually had two bodies. One sacred, one profane; but which was which?

According to the Merriam Webster Dictionary, the term divine right is defined as, "the right of a sovereign to rule as set forth by the theory of government that holds that a monarch receives the right to rule directly from God and not from the people." While this is obviously not how American government derives its authority today, some may argue that certain leaders and their families in American history have used religious affiliation to win the hearts and minds of large segments of the population. Several presidents have used the bible as a reference, a campaign tool, and individuals in government have certainly claimed to have been blessed or received guidance from a divine figure. But divine right should not be used to justify or legitimize the authority of government. We do not worship the state, and if we do worship it like it is a god it will surely destroy us in the name of divine right. Government is manmade; to me the natural way of the planet is divinely ordained. If God created this world, he is not the one who created government, that is the work of Man, and it is evident in its imperfect nature.

God gave this planet to us, the inhabitants of the planet Earth, not to government. Government is not a result of gods will, and no man has the divine right to rule over another man. Government today is a soulless corporation that knows no bounds and makes a rare attempt at being ethically moral. The government is also a tool used by those in powerful positions for their own personal gain; and by powerful corporations and other influences to control the population. Government is a heartless entity that does not trust mankind to be responsible for itself and live in harmony without intervention, coercion, and the use of force to blindly oppress, harass and imprison those it is supposed to serve.

3 "IT'S OUR FAULT BECAUSE WE VOTED FOR THIS GUY."

"The difference between a democracy and a dictatorship is that in a democracy you vote first and take orders later; in a dictatorship you don't have to waste your time voting". **- Charles Bukowski**

It's always easy to blame the current president for the nation's problems, and we've all heard someone complain about the president at one time or another. But the reality is that he is not to blame. The blame can be placed squarely on us, the citizens, and on our unwillingness to reform or abolish an outdated voting system.

The electoral battle staged every four years is meant to equate two presidential candidates as polar opposites. As rhetorical wars are fought and bought with corporate money, the truly substantive issues are never brought up because both teams have a vested interest in the statist quo.

Neither red nor blue candidate ever exhibits uncertainties

concerning more than a century of American imperialism with over 700 military bases spanning the globe, or that this country spends more than the next 19 largest spenders combined on the military-industrial-congressional complex. Instead, they bicker over social issues like an individual's right to marry whomever they want, and if the public should be allowed to keep their guns. In a stateless system, marriage exists outside of the state; but couples don't need state approval to declare their union legitimate.

The corporation-state is the dominant institution of modernity. The logic of state necessity and inevitability rests upon many uninvestigated premises. These assumptions must be interrogated; otherwise court-intellectuals and demagogue-pundits distract us by dramatically rearranging deck-chairs on the Titanic. As Noam Chomsky wrote, "The smart way to keep people passive and obedient is to strictly limit the spectrum of acceptable opinion, but allow very lively debate within that spectrum."

The media always drum up the race as the most important election in history. Those that actually study the history of politics realize that platforms have been blending and triangulating—moving unceasingly in the direction of statism. Left and right may polarize, but they share essential authoritarian characteristics. For example, both candidates favored the National Defense Authorization Act – which strips Americans of their right to a trial before jury and allows for indefinite detainment. Additionally, both parties are beholden to the dictates of the financial sector, empowered and cartelized by the Federal Reserve. Being forced to choose between two candidates is like deciding to poison the well with either arsenic or cyanide; innocent people die either way.

Obama authorized the drone killing of Anwar al-Aulaqi (a United States citizen living in Yemen) in September 2011. The CIA killed his 16 year old son two weeks later. There was no due process – the President unilaterally assassinated a US citizen on foreign soil. And more recently at home, Christopher Dorner, a former cop on the run from the LAPD, was a target of airborne drones operating above U.S. soil.

If any individual killed another person, it would be a heinous crime. When a state kills someone, it's for the greater good and often remains secret for supposed "reasons of national security." Is there no such thing as a fair trial anymore? Even accused killers deserve their day in court.

Any military age male (18-35) is considered a militant by the U.S. army unless proven otherwise. According to the Bureau of Investigative Journalism, from 2004 to 2012, between 2,562 and 3,325 people were killed in drone strikes in Pakistan alone. The U.S. also operates drones in Afghanistan, Iraq, Yemen and Somalia. Some 474 to 881 of those killed in Pakistan were civilians, including 176 children. Another 1,300 were wounded. These numbers are likely to be low, because the U.S. and Pakistani governments seek to obfuscate the severity of the carnage.

Why should we give more power to the guys with the guns and expect that to solve our problems? We must dig to the root of the issue, which is state-capitalism itself; or the economic system where state power protects illegitimate ownership claims and creates artificial scarcity to protect profits. The state is what makes capitalism (but not markets) possible.

The state and the capitalist class are not antagonistic forces, and America is nowhere near a "free market." Big business hates authentically free markets – capitalists prefer mercantilism. Unless you are member of the ruling class, you should do everything you can to bring about a less violent, non-statist paradigm—because states have a nasty tendency to start putting certain people in camps and you never know who will be next.

This resolve has led to a new wave of projects, and to countless books, seminars and YouTube videos promoting freedom. Too bad more are not aware that this chilling political environment we are feeling now is only the beginning of the biting cold of statism.

The genius of President Obama is that the "goodies" of his socialistic healthcare program came before the election, while the "pain" will come after. Today we need work even harder to make the moral case for free markets, non-aggression, and voluntaryism. Today, the American Way is not the popular way. Like our Founding Fathers before us, we are counted as a small band of underground extremist rebels for believing in freedom.

Why must we choose between only the two candidates each election? Suppose someone likes a Libertarian or Green party candidate more than a choice between a donkey and an elephant. They well know that if they were to vote for a minority group, their vote would be wasted unless it's for a candidate in a district where that party is polling better than 25%. This has been coined voting for the "lesser of two evils" but what many fail to realize that a vote for the lesser of two evils, is still a vote for evil. Many voters assume that this problem is an inherent fact of democracy, but it is not. A major defect rests squarely on the U.S.'s archaic election system.

A simple immediate, yet not extremely overwhelming improvement could be; perhaps instead of selecting just one candidate, our voting machines should allow voters to answer "yes or no" to each of the candidates. Then the candidate with the most support would win. This would safely allow someone to vote for a Libertarian candidate, as well as a zoo animal, without any chance of wasting votes or spoiling an election. Such a system allows for any number of candidates, and has even been reported to increase voter turnout by as much as 50%.

It is truly sad to hear people talk about who they voted for and ridiculous for them to actually think that their needs would have been served if they guy they voted for had been elected. With the majority of Americans thinking erroneously that we live in a Democracy, they tend to really take satisfaction that they are doing their part by blindly obliging their civic duty while they are programmed to believe that it is their only way to change things. I love it when I am told; "Well if you don't like it, you should have voted differently", or "If you want to change something you don't like about government, vote to change the laws." Really? Does one person really stand a chance at changing an election with one vote? Is voting for "the other guy" really in your best interest either, and the only alternative? That reasoning is absurd. As far as choosing a qualified presidential candidate, there is no way that you would be able to agree one hundred percent on every issue or even on very many of the important issues, because the important issues will never be addressed the way things are now with the media's designated red or blue option that you are presented with. Plus, lately it is harder and harder to tell the difference between them anyway. They all seem to play for the same team (but they wear different colors), and it doesn't seem to be the home team anymore.

Another important consideration to make is when you register to vote. If you do not support the government and it's coercive, unethical, immoral, and corrupt corporate monopoly, why would you register to vote and legitimize the violence and power of the corporation even more? Registering to vote is locking you into an agreement with, and tacitly justifying the perpetuation of fraudulent actions of government and also the incremental amputation of rights that the government is surgically extracting from its citizens. If the government wants my support, it needs to make some very significant changes at a fundamental level. Changes that I doubt it could ever make without going out of business first.

The United States is a corporation or actually a collection of corporations (It is true, if you do not believe me refer to Title 28 USC Section 3002(5) Chapter 176: United States - US- U.S.-USA-America (a possession of the Queen of England) Means: (A) a federal corporation . . . Title 28 USC Section 3002(5) Chapter 176. It is clear that the United States . . . is a corporation . . . 534 FEDERAL SUPPLEMENT 724. `It is well settled that "United States" et al is a corporation, originally incorporated February 21, 1871 under the name "District of Columbia," 16 Stat. 419 Chapter 62. It was reorganized June 11, 1878; a bankrupt organization per House Joint Resolution 192 on June 5, 1933, Senate Report 93-549, and Executive Orders 6072, 6102, and 6246; a de facto (define de facto) government, originally the ten square mile tract ceded by Maryland and Virginia and comprising Washington D. C., plus the possessions, territories, forts, and arsenals.), and it is also a corporation which I choose to not work for or represent in any capacity, so why would I want to vote for new corporate policy or a new CEO or CFO? The significance of this is that, as a corporation, the United States has no more authority to implement its laws against "We The People" than does the

McDonald's or Wal-Mart corporations. The same reasoning can be used if there was a soft drink company that provided a product in which was used human embryonic kidney cell derivatives and called them flavor enhancers. Would you support such a company? Would you buy their products? Would you contract with them? Would you purchase stock in the company? Would you vote for the CEO? How about a company that specialized in human trafficking, violence, war, and slavery?

Plus if you look into how the votes are tallied (when done honestly), your single vote truly doesn't matter because the popular vote is does not determine the outcome, Electoral College votes do. The result of this system is that your presidential vote doesn't carry nearly as much weight as do your state and local votes. The "Electoral College" allows state legislatures to divide up and allocate votes as they see fit. Not to mention the amount of suspected voter fraud and other election trickery, it is a wonder we still put up with any of it.

This country has had a long history of voting fraud, about which whole novels can be written, but here are a few examples:

When precinct workers in the 1974 Dade County elections discovered that the voting machines they were using were rigged, they walked off the job and refused to certify the election process. Police and fire fighters took over the polling duties. The next day, the Miami Herald reported the walk out, but not the reason. When the precinct workers went to the media to report the election rigging, the media ignored them. So did the local attorney general. So did the FBI. Citizens who tried to observe the next election were arrested for disturbing the peace.

In 1997, the respected Washington, DC publication, The Hill, confirmed that Republican Senator Chuck Hagel was the head, and continues to own part of, ES&S - the company that has installed and programmed nearly half the voting machines used in the United States.

In 2002, Diebold systems supplied the state of Georgia with electronic voting machines. In that election, the incumbent Democratic Governor Ray Barnes was defeated, giving the Republicans their first victory there in 134 years. The poll results showed a miraculous 12-point shift in the last 48 hours. Diebold was subsequently sued for applying a last-minute code patch to the machines that was never reviewed and was also, coincidentally, deleted just after the election.

In April, 2004 California's Voting Systems and Procedures Panel, by an 8-0 vote, recommended that California cease the use of certain Diebold machines.

30% of all votes in the 2004 elections will be tabulated by electronic machines that don't have vote-verification systems.

It would be a minor task to develop public, open-source devices that use military-grade encryption, and employ modern vote-verification technologies. Australia already uses such a system, and many local elections use these systems. (It's important to use open-source code so that the machine's operation and security can be scrutinized by the public for possible flaws and biases. This would also save taxpayers money.)

Why are our voting machines owned and operated by private companies? Perhaps it's because the people in charge got there using an old, corruptible system and they have no interest in changing to a new fair and open system. Or perhaps it's simply because there's a lack of public interest and support for reform.

Nevertheless, when a voting system is so severely broken in all these ways, it's hard to blame the leaders who got promoted by it.

We really do not choose who makes the rules anymore. The majority of voters choose who represents them in voting whether a 1000+ page document he or she can't possibly have read moves up to the next committee. The person they vote in is a politician, a kind of person known far and wide as someone who will lie to get sent to the legislature.

Voting is just a way to make you feel like you are a part of the process, a way to keep you complacent. It is a way to help you to cognitively dismiss complaints about the system; how can you complain if the guy that you voted for took advantage of you again, after all you voted for him! Even if you didn't vote for whoever won you still participated, and by participating in the process you are implicitly supporting the outcome. This is why there will never be a candidate whose views differ from those presented in the mainstream; voting doesn't change anything. The candidates are selected, bought and paid for before a single individual votes either for or against them. It just allows the corporation to have a new front man, a new face on the same old tired and obsolete control mechanism, and then it's just business as usual for another four years.

Even if we did choose who makes the rules, we do not decide what the rules actually are. There is no way to opt out of the government. It will punish us for breaking the rules whether we agree with them or not, whether we voted or not, whether our candidate was elected or not, and whether we know the rules or not.

The most callow, naive, juvenile, inane, and foolish hypothesis, is the hypothesis that governments and violent monopolies exist to assist, aid, protect, and help you. In reality, governments are nothing more than a collection of individuals seeking their own self-interest through threats of violence, and in almost every case, it is in their self-interest to point laws and/or guns *at* you.

During slavery if a slave tried to run away the other slaves would look at him in contempt believing the runaway slave was stealing himself. This was because all of the other slaves firmly believed in the slave masters right to rule.

How could one slave master control one-hundred slaves? The master is out numbered, a hundred to one. When you find the answer to the previous question, you will have the answer to how a hundred thousand IRS agents and five hundred or so politicians control a hundred million taxpayers.

If all people care about is getting a nicer slave master...what possible interest would they have in being truly free? If I wanted a nice slave master I would have chosen Ron Paul. I bet he would be a really nice slave master and would treat me good. But that is not good enough for me and it shouldn't be good enough for the rest of humanity. If people need to beg their masters to be nicer here and beg them not to steal so much from us, then we are NOT truly free in our own minds.

I do not believe we will have a stateless society in my lifetime but I know it will happen. Eventually we will evolve out of this outdated involuntary racket. We need to just get off of this train of thought that we need to restore the old clunker and amending and patching it; we should just buy a new car, or maybe even several new cars... a different style and color (locality) to suit each person's individual taste. As long as we quit repeating the same old failed one-size-fits-all societal structure of the past, and agree to adopt the non-aggression axiom. Would we be able to prevent a cancer from growing just because we happen to write CONSTITUTION on it? We need to address the cause; not just keep medicating the symptoms.

The bill of rights gives us freedom the government can't take away. Is the constitution a god who shoots lightning at those who break its rules? No, of course it isn't. It's just a document. Our rights depend on our ability and willingness to fight for them. The bill of rights is not a list of rights the constitution grants us. It's a list of rights all people have by virtue of their very existence that the government cannot take away without deserving to be overthrown. That's why the 2nd amendment is there. It states the necessity of the people to organize into militias to ensure that the government does not become tyrannical, which it WILL do if the people don't keep it in check. The people aren't doing that, so look what's happening. The bill of rights serves two purposes: to tell the government what it can't do and to tell the people what to do when the government breaks the agreement. If you have any respect for the constitution, you must actively stop supporting it and start using civil disobedience. It's your responsibility to your fellow countrymen and to future generations.

4 "MONOPOLIES WOULD ABOUND WITHOUT GOVERNMENT."

First of all, the government, by virtue is a monopoly so this statement really makes no sense. Second of all ... quick ... name me one monopoly in history that occurred without government support? Not very easy is it? If you think of one, let me know via the website ... I will be here waiting.

Let's look at some of the more well-known monopolies; the Bar has a complete monopoly on lawyers, the DMV has a complete monopoly over automobiles and driver licensure, the American Medical Association has a complete monopoly over doctor licensing, the government supports the complete monopoly that the Federal Reserve has on currency, the Food and Drug Administration, the police, the Courts, the post office, the A.T.F, FEMA, Homeland Security, and the list goes on and on. All of them government supported or run, not to mention subsidized organizations and individuals.

What is the one thing all of those government monopolies have in common? Their services all suck and their prices are highway robbery (ok, I guess that was two things). But, now do you see how ridiculous it is to think that the state cares about protecting you from monopolies?

Just for entertainment, let's say it is completely possible for monopolies to form in a free market. What's the worst they could do? Do you think that a 'free-market' monopoly (funny even saying that) would charge outrageous prices for their products? If people had a choice would a 'free-market' monopoly provide bad service? Would they be able to retain their status as a monopoly if they provided a shoddy overpriced product or service within a voluntary trade environment? Especially if people had a choice and someone else could provide a higher quality product for a lower price? I doubt it. What if they not only charged outlandish prices and provided crappy service, but they could also force you to pay for them? Wait a second, only government is allowed to do that.

Some statists believe that without government intervention, reliance on free markets would lead to a few big firms selling everything. Governments can — and all too often do — give monopolies to favored individuals or groups; that is, they prohibit others from entering the market and competing for the custom of customers. That's what a monopoly means. The monopoly may be granted to a government agency itself (as in the monopolized postal services in many countries) or it may be granted to a favored corporation, association, household, or person.

Do free markets promote monopolization? There's little or no good reason to think so and many reasons to think not. Free markets rest on the freedom of persons to enter the market, to exit the market, and to buy from or sell to whomever they please. If companies in markets with freedom of entry make above average profits, those profits attract rivals to compete those profits away. Some of the literature of economics offers descriptions of hypothetical situations in which certain market conditions could lead to persistent "rents," that is, income in excess of opportunity cost, defined as what the resources could earn in other uses. But concrete examples are extremely hard to find, other than relatively uninteresting cases such as ownership of unique resources (for example, a painting by Rembrandt). In contrast, the historical record is simply full of examples of governments granting special privileges to their supporters.

Freedom to enter the market, and freedom to choose what to buy, and from whom, promote consumer interests by eating away at the temporary market share that the first ones offering a good or service may enjoy. In contrast, endowing governments with power to determine who may or may not provide goods and services creates the monopolies — the actual, historically observed monopolies — that are harmful to consumers and that restrain the productive forces of mankind on which human betterment rests. If markets routinely led to monopolies, we would not expect to see so many people going to government to grant them monopolies at the expense of their less powerful competitors and customers. They could get their monopolies through the market, instead.

It's always worth remembering that government itself seeks to exercise a monopoly; it's a classic defining characteristic of a government that it exercises a monopoly based upon the exercise of force in a given geographic area. Why should we expect such a monopoly to be friendlier to competition than the market itself, which is defined by the freedom to compete?

Critics of truly free markets tend to see monopolies everywhere, even where no one else sees a monopoly, and statists often do not see monopolies, even when one seemingly exists. But there is a reason why a seeming monopoly is often not a real monopoly. Suppose one large business smelts all the aluminum, as in fact right now it does. Provided there is nothing that stops anyone else from smelting aluminum, what is the harm in that? This would only be a problem if no one else could smelt aluminum. So the aluminum monopoly may look like a monopoly, but really it is not, for it can only keep its "monopoly" by keeping prices low and quality high.

Suppose on the other hand, one big landlord owned all the land, or owned land surrounding every person's land and claimed the right to prevent passage, and enforced his will. Then that would indeed be a monopoly. That big landlord would have the power of a socialist state, would in fact be a socialist state, and people would be right to rebel against that state, kill its rulers, and redistribute the state's property to individuals.

If a real monopoly, not what statists call a monopoly, but a true monopoly occurs, then all the statist arguments against socialism and justifying violence against statist measures apply to that monopoly, and if that monopoly dresses itself in the clothes of property rights and voluntary agreements, then all the statist arguments against property rights and voluntary agreements apply to the property of that particular monopoly. But when property rights are thus set aside, one always winds up killing people. Before confronting such an alleged monopoly, one needs to ask: should we be killing people, or should we be seeking an alternate source of these goods?

In many cases, to ask the question is to answer it. The so called monopoly is usually no monopoly at all.

5 "YOU HAVE A SOCIAL CONTRACT, THAT'S WHY."

The Social Contract theory holds that a population in a given territory agrees to contract some of their inherent power to government as needed to promote the well-being of all. People lived poorly and to improve their lives people could enter into a social contract where a superior person would rule over the rest.

How often has a statist made the argument? "The social contract means that because you live here, under this government you automatically agree to obey." Really? So that's it? The state is legitimate because a non-existent, or perhaps fraudulent at best, contract that no one can produce says so?

I have already many a time discussed and written about the problems with this argument but that doesn't seem to convince the state worshippers. I've even pointed out how this is a completely wild card argument you could use to justify literally *anything* a government does. Is anyone seriously going to try and tell me that the holocaust was perfectly justified because if the Jews didn't approve, they should have moved away or voted in someone else? I'm not comparing anyone to Nazis. I'm simply saying that the argument is so open ended that it could be used to justify the Nazis and that's why it fails and that's why it seems that statists just need to think their arguments through a little more carefully before they parrot something they heard on TV.

What kind of perversion of thought does it take to make such a completely illogical, baseless, freedom-hating, hypocritical non-argument look like a valid point?

The truth is this; governments only made semi-logical sense back when people used to believe in the divine right of kings. Since the king was supposedly directly chosen by god, that was proof that he should rule and allowed him to take exception to all of god's rules. It makes sense that a person's dedication to their religion insured obedience. In a way a sort of back up method to insure compliance with the crown, that could make some kind of sense if you accepted the premise that God exists, and that he has given a divine right to your ruler.

Jean-Jacques Rousseau was one of the most influential of the Enlightenment philosophers. Born in Geneva in 1712, he spent much of his adult life in Paris, where he became involved with the philosophes of the Enlightenment and began to write his own philosophical works. Rousseau is best known for *"The Social Contract"* in which he states that society and government are really a "contract" between men. Even he admits that no government truly has a right to rule without the agreement of those who are ruled. This was a revolutionary thought in an age when kings claimed they ruled by divine right. Rousseau's writings were quoted by French revolutionaries and greatly influenced the thought of Karl Marx.

Rousseau did imply however, that rather than having the divine right of kings, the power was held by the divine right of "crowds" instead. In other words the collective will would be the absolute power and all individuals would sacrifice their individual will over to the collective. If an individual did not comply with the collective then they would be forced to comply. In other words, this amounted to collectivism by force and not a contractual obligation.

This brings us to the biggest problem with the whole social contract theory; in order for there to be a "conscionable" (non-fraudulent, and in good faith) contract there has to be 3 conditions met. Contracts must have full disclosure, valuable consideration and consent. With the "Social Contract" theory none of those conditions are being met; therefore there can be no contract.

For a contract to be conscionable and ultimately enforceable, the terms must be clear to every single person implicated. Every party to the contract has to know the terms, and agree to those terms. You can't just write a contract based on your terms and then expect someone to be in compliance with it ex post facto without their signature and claim that it has power over them.

The act of voting however, could be looked at as entering into a contract and implying an obligation of allegiance to the state. When you register to vote, you could very well be consenting to the 'social contract'. In other words registering to vote could be viewed as you individually giving the corrupt system legitimacy. If you refuse to vote or acknowledge that they have that power over you, then the contract has not been signed. Without there being a legitimate contract there is no presumable right to enforce it. My view is that not all social contracts are bad though. If there was one that was in line with the non-aggression principle, I would give it a fair shake if the terms were acceptable. We do not have the benefit of that though; what we have is a system where people are expected to comply with the will of men who aren't even alive anymore just because we were born. That is not a legitimate agreement. You cannot be born into an agreement that someone else made for you. That is why Thomas Jefferson said that every generation needs to take responsibility for the writing of their own constitution, and not just accept what came before.

The reason the State has come to dominate our lives instead of being the public servant it originated as, is because those who pull the strings of government have manipulated us into acting under commerce, by way of application and registration. The State sees applying as synonymous with begging, and it sees registration as handing over the legal title to whatever is being registered. Thus the State then has your consent in a contract that you didn't even know was one. This however, is fraudulent, as full disclosure was never given with regards to the truth of the registration process. You were duped into believing you had to sign their documents or face fines, possibly even legal action. The State can only get away with this if you agree to represent a fictional legal entity, known as the strawman. Your Government name, in all capitals. This is not you, but an account held in your name. If they can't get you to act on behalf of this fiction, they have no claim of right over your affairs.

I love to ask the statist to make the connection between me and the laws you say apply to me by factually explaining when, where, how, and with whom this "social contract" was agreed upon. Then, define what an informal agreement is. If you cannot do those this, it is all conjecture; your opinion based on whatever non-factual influence made you come to that conclusion.

Simply saying that there are laws in place proves nothing more than the fact that people sat around and made up some rules and wrote them down. It fails to prove how the legislation is binding or that a valid "social contract" was ever created. In a morally proper world no person would be obligated to do anything (other than respect the rights of others) that they have not agreed to.

The social contract claim made by a statist, amounts to nothing more than arguing that a group of people with a monopoly on violence somehow is legitimate, and that you agree to it simply by living in a specific geographic location. That somehow all individuals within a geographic location must abide by the rules of an imaginary contract. Yet they will never be able to explicitly identify the parties involved, when the agreement was made, where the agreement was made, and evidence of the agreement itself. If you cannot do that, your argument is just conjecture.

The social contract argument argument boils down to a small group of people, whom cannot be identified in any way, forced a larger group of people into a system of rules without their consent or knowledge ... perhaps at birth? Where are the facts to back up any of this? What most of us think of as laws are really statute (another name for corporate policy), and also are nothing but opinions. How do they apply to someone who has not consented? There was no offer, consideration, understanding, or consent. But, the statist is convinced somehow that there is an "informal agreement" which still cannot be defined. They were never offered at any point as terms of an agreement. No one was told that they had been forced onto an agreement. There may be things called laws, but that does not obligate anyone to anything. I can write rules on paper, but if no one agrees to them, they do not apply.

A statist would say that it's an informal agreement or understanding between you and a society. It encompasses all those understandings that are part of being in a society rather than being in the wild - such as the understanding that you will pay for purchases at the cash, rather than burst in and take them by force or sneak off with them, as an animal from the wild would - or people in breach of the social contract do.

But that would mean that the "social contract" is not a contract at all. A contract is a formal agreement. What is an informal agreement? How does one become a member of a society? The statist may concede that it is not based on a geographic area, but not always.

Society, according to the typical statist explanation is nothing more than an arbitrary category. They will mention nothing of a voluntary entrance into it, instead they provide qualities that people have in common.

A society is an arbitrary categorization of people based on what a person believes a group has in common. It is a description, a fiction used to categorize people. It is not based on voluntary entry into a group. Yet the statist would have you believe that once categorized as a person of a society, some kind of an informal agreement (yet to be defined) called a social contract is imposed upon all members of the society and the terms of which (though not known by the members or brought to their attention) must be adhered to.

"If you're in a society, you're in a social contract." That means my geographic location is consent to a contract. Really? This is not a factual argument, where are the facts? It is all conjecture when the statist attempts to explain. If the social contract presumption was factual, it would be able to be shown how, factually, anyone has entered into a social contract with anyone else. Also, who is the other party with whom one would have entered into a contract with? The government? Other people? The only thing we really need to agree upon is the non-aggression principle, and then the rest is up to us.

Just because a group of people write their rules down on paper does not mean that I must be forced to do something that I do not want to do; such as die, be a slave, have my property stolen, or be under constant surveillance.

Maybe the statist will say that we all entered into the social contract upon birth. So in other words, my parents, unknowingly, entered me into an agreement that I could not have possibly have consented to, and also have no knowledge of, and that I have agreed to the terms of the agreement even though i have not been presented with them, that the group doing business as the "government" is the party with which I have entered into the agreement with, that they control all the territory known as the "UNITED STATES OF AMERICA", and that by residing in this territory I somehow imply consent?

That is making a lot of presumptions, many of them ridiculous in merit. How can one presume another is contractually obligated to the thing called the "social contract" without proving the legitimacy of it? Rights cannot be granted, only privileges are. The statist believes we all owe allegiance due to the "social contract", when in fact the state is supposed to gain our allegiance through consent, and morality.

A contract is a binding agreement entered into freely by two or more parties. No contract can be automatic, and no contract can be binding unless it is binding on ALL parties involved; that means one party can't have the option to change the contract without notice, as many often try.

So the biggest flaw in the "social contract" theory is that any agreement made under threat and duress is not legitimate. The "state", having a monopoly on violence, uses force to accomplish ALL of its goals. So saying that I agreed to something because I acquired a driver's license is not accurate. I did it because "government" thugs would use violence against if I did not. A license cannot be granted for an unlawful activity, otherwise that is licensing criminality. This is why it cannot be unlawful to travel without a license, but it can be illegal to drive commercially without one. One is a contractual obligation to obey rules set up by the corporation in exchange of use of the roads to conduct commerce, where the other is a God given right from our creator, and government has no authority to tell us that we may not do it.

I have a right to move about freely. If the government forces me to pay for roads and for the permission to use them, I am not in agreement, I am simply doing what I have to do in order to live comfortably.

How can you enter into an agreement with something that doesn't exist? It does exist, you say... it can put you in jail. Those really are people acting under the color of law and only represent the government. Could you introduce me to the STATE OF OREGON? So if I cannot meet the "STATE OF OREGON" how could the STATE OF OREGON press charges against me? How could the

STATE OF OREGON claim to be a victim? But the funniest thing is when you go to court you can get the STATE's witness to usually admit that you were within the plaintiff at the time of the arrest. How would that work? Being within the plaintiff? See what I mean? The STATE is a fiction. It does not exist. It cannot be the ground because the ground existed before the STATE, and the STATE did not create the ground. So, the government cannot enter into any agreement with people because it factually does not exist. The same logic can be applied to the other "contracts" that statists may claim to have entered into with the "government".

Getting a STATE issued ID or driver's license and working at a job where you provided a SSN and subsequently have them automatically deduct taxes, getting a bank loan, and other such activities are all contracts by consent.

You don't HAVE to do anything as drastic as "renouncing your citizenship" (which you can't do unless you already have established citizenship elsewhere anyway), all you have to do is stay out of debt, stay off the welfare, and conduct yourself responsibly and honorably. Too simple!

What happens if I am caught by government thugs driving on a roadway without a license? Where can I get a job without a social security number? If those jobs exist, are they available in all fields of my interest? If I do not pay taxes, will I have trouble with the government? What are the consequences for not having a social security number?

If you plan to drive on a "public street", without license and registration you need to make sure that you realize that you are indeed responsible for yourself, and if you harm someone or their property you need to be able to make things right. Beware that invalid/expired plates give the government corporate policy enforcers "reasonable suspicion" to pull you over.

By acting responsibly and honorably, you can maximize your societal benefits and minimize hindrance.

A constitution of, for, by, with or of any other type makes no difference. The fact remains that ALL so called social contracts are invalid that are not expressly consented to by all parties involved after receiving full disclosure and the parties being able to legitimately consent to them.

A statist, as a last resort (before name calling and emotionally overreacting) will usually say that the person that wants freedom can opt out of the social contract/informal agreement that was never consented to in the first place, by renouncing "citizenship". The consequences of this are that they would then be trespassing on land that they no longer were welcome on and would have to go some other place not already claimed by a group of people doing business as a "government" (I destroy this argument in chapter 12).

How could you agree to something without the faculty of thought to be able to agree to it? How could you make the mistake of being born somewhere when you don't even have the choice in the first place?

Statists seem to be trying to find some legal loophole that gives the thugs doing business as "the government" a legitimate reason for their actions. If no formal agreement is made, there is no agreement. I do not care what the opinion of a group of people called "the legislator" or another group calling themselves "the judiciary" says. If such an agreement exists, where is it? How and when was it agreed to? What were the terms? Was I given full disclosure?

The "government" makes up any rules it wants to justify the control it has over society. They obtain and maintain it by force. States and statists can both claim that I agreed to something, but neither one can prove it. There are no facts to support that argument. There may be a birth certificate, but that does not prove that I agreed to anything nor did it create an obligation on me. It can also be said that the state provides services, but they do so by way of theft.

I do not voluntarily pay taxes. I do not voluntarily support "government." Because it is compulsory, there can be no contract. Contracts are voluntary agreements. When violence is used to establish an agreement, it is not an agreement.

Allegiance is given in return for protection. But the Supreme Court ruled that there is no duty for the police to provide protection. That eliminates the government's portion of the agreement and causes the whole thing to be void. No protection, no allegiance, no citizens. Also, the idea of tacit consent or an implicit contract makes no sense. There can be no agreement if I did not explicitly agree. They may say otherwise, but they are wrong.

The belief that anything the government says or does that a person does not publicly disagree with or reject equates to acceptance of the other parties terms is ridiculous. So when I ignore someone who is telling me that they are going to assault me or steal my property is agreement that they can do so? Not acknowledging an offer is not the same as accepting it.

Without divine right, all arguments for the state self-detonate. The initiation of violence is bad so we need to give one elite group permission to initiate violence in order to stop the initiation of violence? Even a 5 year old can tell that this reasoning makes no sense.

So while the smart people have gone on to start questioning the premises of the state's existence as a whole, the slower people (and that's the nicest term I can use), desperate to hold onto their dogma simply whipped out a replacement for divine right which came in the form of the social contract. Now instead of "You have to obey because the invisible man in the sky that I can't even prove exists says so" it's "You have to obey because the invisible contract that I can't even prove exists says so." It's nothing more than feeble excuse making for elitism, fascism and barbarism and it needs to stop.

6 "WE DESERVE GOVERNMENT HEALTHCARE."

Thomas Jefferson once said, "Sometimes it is said that man cannot be trusted with the government of himself. Can he, then, be trusted with the government of others?"

Statists will generally agree that government-run health care is inefficient, debt-ridden, coercive, unsustainable, slow and subject to pressure-group influence, and while these are all true the sad fact is that these arguments don't work because people just don't care about proficiency. If the poor have a right to health care, it doesn't matter if it's difficult to provide. It's like telling a a family with a new puppy that puppies will chew up all your socks, eat too much, barks all the time and so on – who cares? They have to take care of their puppy (if they are responsible), and they have a moral obligation to it. From this we can presume that practical arguments never trump arguments from morality.

Insurance in medicine got its start when the government allowed companies to deduct medical costs if they provided their employees with medical insurance. This treated fringe benefits differently than cash payments. So right from the start of this "healthcare" movement, government meddling has been causing problems. Think about other government agencies you interact with (police, court, DMV, IRS etc.), would you want them to also provide your healthcare? Imagine going to the doctor, but they now have an incompetency factor that is reminiscent of going to the DMV. Long lines, slow service, just take a number and someone who hates their job will be with you shortly. Not to worry, this government agency now literally knows you inside and out along with your entire medical history. Of course healthcare providers will be held accountable for mistakes and bad treatment, after all being the only game in town ... after a while there won't be any private provider standard of service anymore. But the good thing is that you probably will never even know the difference, because it will be standardized and implemented everywhere.

The main selling point for government healthcare in the United States is that everyone has a right to health care, but the poor are too much of a burden on the system that they deserve to have healthcare too, but at a third parties expense. In other words all poor are categorized into a group that is unable to care for themselves, and it is up to the non-poor to take care of them. We had better be careful when we create something for the "poor", because then we are not only categorizing and marginalizing people, and once we start down that path we risk ending up being categorized and marginalized ourselves.

As long as the poor are healthy, the government run healthcare owes them nothing. As soon as they get sick however, the doctor (government) now owes him a debt which it is morally obligated to pay off. However, this moral commandment fails the test of universality. Here is a man, and the doctor is a man, and yet they are both subject to opposing moral rules at the same time, since the poor person is now entitled through government to services and the doctor is ethically required to provide them. So in other words, when a poor person gets sick, government healthcare suddenly owes them money, time and resources, without reference to any sort of contract. How can that be resolved? How can two men be subjected to both absolute and opposite moral rules at the same time? Have their fundamental natures changed? If not, then the moral absolute that everyone has a right to health care fails, especially when the resources to provide that supposed "right" is taken by force from someone else.

Theories which claim universal absolutes must also be true without regard for time. Murder cannot be wrong today, but right yesterday. This is clearly not the case with "the poor". One day, they have no right to someone else's time and money. However, the next day, they have an absolute right to them. How severe does an illness have to be for the complete reversal of this moral right to occur? If they have a cold, can they demand treatment at 3am? And does someone even have to be sick? What if someone is just curious about sexually transmitted diseases? Can he drop in for a nice chat with his doctor about that? And if he does, what about the right to health care of everyone else in the government healthcare doctor's waiting room? What degree of need is required to justify forcing the healthcare provider to deliver something he has no moral obligation to provide? Does a cold suffice? What about a minor burn? There really is no objective line that can be drawn. But even if a moral line could be drawn, what about preventative medical care? If someone has a right to health care, then we can assume that they have the right to regular checkups. So they go to the doctor for an exam and they are pronounced perfectly healthy, so the presence of illness cannot be used to claim any applicable moral difference. How then, can these two people who have no other obligation to each other be subjected to absolutely opposite moral rules at the same time and in the same room? The question cannot be answered. If someone has stolen my bicycle, I am completely within my rights to go and get it back, and even using force if necessary. Thus, if a doctor owes his services to anyone who is sick, then hundreds of millions of people have the right to go and extract those services from him, with force if necessary. Does this sound like something people have a moral right to demand?

What about nurses? Receptionists? The janitors who nightly clean up the offices of the insurance companies? The investors who lend money to pharmaceutical companies? The teacher who instructs the computer programmer who writes a medical billing system? What about the babysitter who looks after the kids of the nurse so she can work a night shift? Does the babysitter also 'owe' services to the sick? Can she be sued if she doesn't show up, and the nurse has to cancel her shift? Where can the line be objectively drawn between those who provide health care services and those who do not? Isn't the moral theory of a 'right' to health care obviously foolish, illogical, subjective and unworkable?

When does someone in the process of becoming a doctor switch from a person with a right to receive health care to someone with an obligation to provide it? In other words, since from one day to the next they become subjected to completely opposite moral absolutes, what changes in them? Is it at 12:01am on the day they see their first patient? Is that when they flip into this alternate and opposite moral universe? Think about how silly this is as a moral theory – 12:00am, they are owed health care – 12:01am, they owe health care to everyone else.

If people have a right to health care, then can the doctor ever take a vacation? Can he retire? Is he obligated to answer health questions while on vacation? What if he doesn't? What if he decides to quit medicine and become an astronaut? Is he no longer required to provide health care? Why not? What has changed? How can moral rules switch so randomly for the same person? How can this be called any kind of consistent and logical moral theory?

Cloaked in the mysterious fog of government force, the problem of individual use of violence is bypassed and buried in emotional rhetoric. So let's take that as an axiom, and say that the government has the right to take Joe taxpayer's money and give it to our poor sick person the doctor – or even just pay the doctor directly after the poor sick patient visits him. What could be wrong with that?

Well, nothing at all – except that the above is a mere description of the uses of violence, and has nothing to do with any moral theory whatsoever. If I say that stealing is wrong for everyone, that's a moral theory. If I say that stealing is wrong for everyone except for people named 'Sam' between the hours of nine to five, I've expressed a random and rather silly opinion, not a moral theory. If I say that everyone has a right to health care, that's a moral theory which can be examined rationally – however, if I say that some people have a right to limited degrees of health care under certain circumstances, and that only certain other people have a right to procure that by the use of force while acting in a different (government) capacity, and then only to a certain degree, and that doctors must provide health care, unless they're on vacation, or it's after 5pm, and so on and blah de blah – then that's not any sort of moral theory, but just a bunch of silly and self-contradictory statements that don't even add up to a coherent subjective opinion, let alone a consistent and objective proposition. It would be like proposing a scientific theory which says that sometimes rocks fall up, and sometimes they fall down – and sometimes they fall up and down (and sideways!) at the same time! A person proposing such a theory invites a prescription for medication far more than a rational response.

Opposing the consequences of government programs has no effect – as we have seen for decades – if people believe that government programs are moral. If someone claims a moral absolute, they must be responsible enough to know what they are talking about. A moral absolute puts guns on the street – it puts people in jail, and sets the whole machinery of state violence in unstoppable motion. If you meet a man who advocates the use of violence to solve social or economic problems, you must insist that he must submit his moral premises to rigorous and relentless logical examination – if he does not, then he is just calling for universal violence to enforce his opinions, which is a very great evil.

The scariest thought is not morality or inefficiencies in care though, but how the doctor's choices for your treatments will actually be the government's choices, or at least heavily influenced by them. With government mandated healthcare, there likely will be no more "second opinions" as far a diagnosis and treatment, as the government will not be able to afford any unneeded expended resources or treatments. Simply the fact that the insurance company has a middleman relationship between you and your healthcare provider means that there will be many decisions made that will be decisions based on budget and other factors that you would normally not consider to be at issue in a private system, and they will not be decisions you get to make the majority of the time.

The insurance company has an established relationship with healthcare providers, and introducing government regulation will not help. After all, each is another organization that has been instituted to control those in control, and each is also another corporation that needs to make a profit. A few cost-cutting measures will surely be innovative, while many others will be sacrifices.

The truth of the matter is that the US medical system is a huge complicated and shameful mess when it comes to the real reason why a medical system should exist, and that is to provide people with the basic right of having access to decent medical care. Trying to regulate this mess into success is like trying to win a marathon by slipping the competition a sleeping pill. Sure, you might win, but how will you know how well you did with no competition?

Another issue is that of choice; in the past if you had a doctor that didn't want to provide a particular treatment, under the private system you could "shop" for someone who would. I am sure that doctor shopping will not be covered by the insurance companies and government regulated healthcare, as it would never be considered to be cost effective.

What about those who do not want the government meddling in what they consider their private affairs that pertain to healthcare? Will anyone be able to opt-out? It is wrong to be forced to pay for something that an individual doesn't want to pay for. Will a black market for healthcare ensue?

What if the government deems that the population needs to be reduced or deeming that a certain element of the population that does not agree with the system has a condition that needs to be treated. With the IRS acting as the collection agency for the new collective government run healthcare system, will people who owe back taxes be denied care?

What about the long history our government has of running experiments on unsuspecting members of society? Could we honestly expect them to be moral and ethical in their treatment of us after the other horrifying things that they have done to unsuspecting victims in the past? For your convenience, I have listed some examples below.

In 1932 the Tuskegee experiments are initiated, in which 200 black men diagnosed with syphilis are never told of their illness, they are then denied treatment, and instead are used as human guinea pigs in order to follow the progression and symptoms of the disease. They all subsequently die from syphilis; their families never told that they could have been treated.

In 1942 Chemical Warfare Services ran mustard gas experiments on approximately 4,000 servicemen. The experiments continue until 1945 and made use of Seventh Day Adventists who chose to become human guinea pigs rather than serve on active duty.

In 1946 Patients in VA hospitals are used as guinea pigs for medical experiments. In order to allay suspicions, the order is given to change the word "experiments" to "investigations" or "observations" whenever reporting a medical study performed in one of the nation's veteran's hospitals.

In 1947 Colonel E.E. Kirkpatrick of the U.S. Atomic Energy Commission issues a secret document (Document 07075001, January 8, 1947) stating that the agency will begin administering intravenous doses of radioactive substances to human subjects. In 1947 the CIA also begins its study of LSD as a potential weapon for use by American intelligence. Human subjects (both civilian and military) are used with and without their knowledge.

In 1950 Department of Defense begins plans to detonate nuclear weapons in desert areas and monitor downwind residents for medical problems and mortality rates. Also, in 1950 in an experiment to determine how susceptible an American city would be to biological attack, the U.S. Navy sprays a cloud of bacteria from ships over San Francisco. Monitoring devices are situated throughout the city in order to test the extent of infection. Many residents become ill with pneumonia-like symptoms. And in 1951 the Department of Defense begins open air tests using disease-producing bacteria and viruses. Tests last through 1969 and there was concern that people in the surrounding areas had been exposed.

In 1953 the CIA initiates Project MKULTRA. This is an eleven year research program designed to produce and test drugs and biological agents that would be used for mind control and behavior modification. Six of the subprojects involved testing the agents on unwitting human beings. And in 1955 the Army Chemical Corps uses LSD research to study its potential use as a chemical incapacitating agent. More than 1,000 Americans participate in the tests, which continue until 1958. Then in 1960 The Army Assistant Chief-of-Staff for Intelligence (ACSI) authorizes field testing of LSD in Europe and the Far East. Testing of the European population is code named Project THIRD CHANCE;

testing of the Asian population is code named Project DERBY HAT.

In 1956 U.S. military released mosquitoes infected with Yellow Fever over Savannah, Georgia and Avon Park, Florida. After each test, army agents posing as public health officials test victims for effects.

In 1965 Project CIA and Department of Defense begin Project MKSEARCH, a program to develop a capability to manipulate human behavior through the use of mind-altering drugs.

In 1965 Prisoners at the Holmesburg State Prison in Philadelphia are subjected to dioxin, the highly toxic chemical component of Agent Orange used in Viet Nam. The men are later studied for development of cancer, which indicates that Agent Orange had been a suspected carcinogen all along.

In 1966 the CIA initiates Project MKOFTEN, a program to test the toxicological effects of certain drugs on humans and animals.

1969 Dr. Robert MacMahan of the Department of Defense requests from congress $10 million to develop within 5 to 10 years, a synthetic biological agent to which no natural immunity exists. And in 1970 funding for the synthetic biological agent is obtained under H.R. 15090. The project, under the supervision of the CIA, is carried out by the Special Operations Division at Fort Detrick, the army's top secret biological weapons facility. Speculation is raised that molecular biology techniques are used to produce AIDS-like retroviruses.

In 1970 the United States intensifies its development of "ethnic weapons" (Military Review, Nov., 1970), designed to selectively target and eliminate specific ethnic groups who are susceptible due to genetic differences and variations in DNA.

In 1975 the virus section of Fort Detrick's Center for Biological Warfare Research is renamed the Fredrick Cancer Research Facilities and placed under the supervision of the National Cancer Institute (NCI) . It is here that a special virus cancer program is initiated by the U.S. Navy, purportedly to develop cancer-causing viruses. It is also here that retro virologists isolate a virus to which no immunity exists. It is later named HTLV (Human T-cell Leukemia Virus).

In 1978 experimental Hepatitis B vaccine trials, conducted by the CDC, begin in New York, Los Angeles and San Francisco. Ads for research subjects specifically ask for promiscuous homosexual men.

In 1981 first cases of AIDS are confirmed in homosexual men in New York, Los Angeles and San Francisco, triggering speculation that AIDS may have been introduced via the Hepatitis B vaccine

In 1985 according to the journal Science (227:173-177), HTLV and VISNA, a fatal sheep virus, are very similar, indicating a close taxonomic and evolutionary relationship. And in 1986 According to the Proceedings of the National Academy of Sciences (83:4007-4011), HIV and VISNA are highly similar and share all structural elements, except for a small segment which is nearly identical to HTLV. This leads to speculation that HTLV and VISNA may have been linked to produce a new retrovirus to which no natural immunity exists.

In 1986 A report to Congress reveals that the U.S. Government's current generation of biological agents includes: modified viruses, naturally occurring toxins, and agents that are altered through genetic engineering to change immunological character and prevent treatment by all existing vaccines.

In 1987 Department of Defense admits that, despite a treaty banning research and development of biological agents, it continues to operate research facilities at 127 facilities and universities around the nation.

1990 More than 1500 six-month old black and Hispanic babies in Los Angeles are given an "experimental" measles vaccine that had never been licensed for use in the United States. CDC later admits that parents were never informed that the vaccine being injected to their children was experimental.

In 1994, with a technique called "gene tracking," Dr. Garth Nicolson at the MD Anderson Cancer Center in Houston, TX discovers that many returning Desert Storm veterans are infected with an altered strain of Mycoplasma incognitus, a microbe commonly used in the production of biological weapons. Incorporated into its molecular structure is 40 percent of the HIV protein coat, indicating that it had been man-made.

In 1994 senator John D. Rockefeller issues a report revealing that for at least 50 years the Department of Defense has used hundreds of thousands of military personnel in human experiments and for intentional exposure to dangerous substances. Materials included mustard and nerve gas, ionizing radiation, psychochemicals, hallucinogens, and drugs used during the Gulf War.

In 1995 U.S. Government admits that it had offered Japanese war criminals and scientists who had performed human medical experiments salaries and immunity from prosecution in exchange for data on biological warfare research.

In 1995 Dr. Garth Nicolson, uncovers evidence that the biological agents used during the Gulf War had been manufactured in

Freedom *from* Government: Statist Delusions

Houston, Texas and Boca Raton, Florida and tested on prisoners in the Texas Department of Corrections. And then in 1996 the Department of Defense admits that Desert Storm soldiers were exposed to chemical agents.

With a history like this (and there were many more, this is just a few), who isn't scared to death of letting their government provide them healthcare?

Today, we are constantly being told, the United States faces a health care crisis. Medical costs are too high, and health insurance is out of reach of the poor. The cause of this crisis is never made very clear, but the cure is made obvious to everybody: government must step in to solve the problem.

On the other side of the coin, could someone be denied healthcare for not wanting to support the government in other ways, such as not volunteering to pay taxes? Would these people have to somehow find their healthcare on the black market? Or would they just suffer? What if you just wanted to pay for your own healthcare and did not believe in supporting the bloated bureaucratic insurance scam of a healthcare system we seemed to have enveloped ourselves in? We must realize that we cannot rely on government to be responsible for keeping us healthy.

Finally, allowing government to be involved in managing healthcare is the perfect opportunity for the government to become intimate with more of our personal information; from tax records, now tied to healthcare records, matched up to Facebook profiles, bank accounts, and more. All this information categorized and data mined, stored and will likely be made available to every other government run enterprise into a virtual inescapable mega-profile about each of us. The computer may also determine the best course of action and the perfect diagnosis for each of us as well. Perhaps someday it will even be legislated that law enforcement can have access to medical records when they pull up a person's record on their computer during a traffic stop. Then they would know if they are dealing with one of those people that need to be treated for an anti-statist mental "condition", it will be administered in the best interest of the subject, of course.

7 "THE ECONOMY WOULD COLLAPSE WITHOUT GOVERNMENT REGULATION."

This is one of those statements that a statist will say that has no basis in fact at all. It is so general and broad that there is no way they could know if it is really a true statement. There has always been a government in this country and it has always more or less regulated business here in the United States so there is no way that a statist could even know if the economy really would collapse without government. I think that local geographic territories could be formed, and they each could create their own rules for trade. Perhaps then we could experiment with alternatives to the current system and find one or more that work well on a bigger scale.

It is sad to see things like kids getting their lemonade stands shut down by police for not having a permit, government trying to regulate what we can sell at garage sales, and organic farmers getting raided for selling raw milk. Seems like there are more and more instances where people are having problems with government interfering in free trade and that is wrong in my opinion. We also do not need government "protecting" us from a myriad of substances, products, and technologies so they can make more money and maintain their monopoly on them. I think that we need to find a way to enforce morality or at least discourage immorality within corporations (including government) so that they have a reason to stay away from implementing practices that are harmful to the planet or to people. We need to somehow separate the rights of corporations from those of people, because the risk for acting immorally and having immunity through the corporation is something that happens quite frequently today. We need to prevent or discourage corporations from being able to do things like; performing harmful testing on people, polluting, or plundering natural resources.

We also need to find a way to bring back innovation and make it easy to allow people to make a living for themselves. There are so many hurdles and obstacles to starting a business in this economy, we need to remove these difficulties so that people are not intimidated from starting their own business and it is feasible financially as well.

Just as the corporations need to find a moral base, we do too. If we could all live by the right moral principles somehow and realize that we each need to be responsible for ourselves individually, collectively the world would definitely be a better place to live. We must also realize that part of being responsible for ourselves means that we are able to also allow others to be just as responsible for themselves without being violent or coercive towards them according to the non-aggression principle.

Simply put, government coercion short-circuits the ability of voluntary cooperation to work. In other words, the government you're counting on to fix the problems is getting in the way. They're not only failing to solve the problems, but they are the problems.

Another huge problem with the economy is the fact that the institution that regulates monetary policy in the United States is "privately owned". The Federal Reserve controls the entire supply of currency and loans currency at interest to the United States government. They have the sole right to print money and "lend" it to the government in the United States. The dollars that the Federal Reserve prints also are not backed by anything of value, And they are actively working to devalue it even more with quantitative easing. Their solution seems to be to just print enough money to pay off all of our debts. So what if the cost of a roll of toilet paper jumps to $50? We'll just print more money. Why can't the US government print its own money? Why can't the government just lend the money directly to the people that needed the loans; the end consumer? We need to cut out the middleman that is the Federal Reserve, it is time for its bubble to finally burst.

The role of the government is to create and maintain conditions conducive to private economic prosperity. In other words: The role of the government is to prevent the mess. If it could not even do that, it is unlikely that the government will be able to fix it now. Indeed, policies currently being undertaken are likely to create new problems of their own, such as the excessive amount of debt, the debasing of the US dollar, and the misallocation of resources resulting from propping up failed businesses at the expense of viable ones.

Government regulation in the economy should be more like

placement of a stop sign at a busy intersection or a rule that was meant to prevent individuals from behaving dishonestly, not to make it difficult to trade freely or encourage monopolies through subsidies and other backing. To an extent, regulation does serve as a device that limits activities of people in the marketplace. However, the implication that statists make is wrong: they believe that without government regulation in economic activity, the economy itself would erupt into chaos.

That is untrue on two counts. First, one must differentiate regulation (which often is specific to a certain area of business) from law (which is more general). For example, there are laws against fraud, and long before governments began to regulate the US economy, people brought alleged fraud cases to court, as well as other tort action that existed under a common law system. Thus, the allegations that without government regulation, there would be no legal oversight of markets are untrue.

The second misconception is that there are no self-regulatory aspects of individual behavior in a market setting. This does not only mean a belief that there are no self-policing mechanisms, but also that markets operate on the edge of chaos. This is patently untrue. Because private enterprise works on a voluntary basis, a business owner cannot coerce someone to do business with him. Things like loss of reputation, shoddy products, poor service and the like serve as real boundaries for business owners, who in a free market survive only by offering goods that people are willing to purchase.

Moreover, there are numerous private (meaning voluntary) organizations that police businesses, settle disputes, independently test products, and provide needed information for consumers and producers alike. Yes, these organizations do have a regulating effect upon the behavior of individuals who participate in private production and exchange. Thus, the statist claim that without government, markets would be a chaotic mess is simply untrue.

Given the reality that markets are self-regulating, how did the US economy (not to mention economies of other nations) become a morass of hundreds of thousands of state, local, and federal regulations that govern things to the minutest detail? Furthermore, why have we not seen a revolt of business owners and consumers alike, who ultimately pay the price for the modern regulatory state? The answer is both simple— and complex.

Regulation is like inflation; both are portrayed as bad things, both are products of the state, yet they persist. And they persist because at least some influential individuals are benefiting from them. Thus, those who gain are going to make sure that these issues are portrayed in the most favorable light.

When politicians, economists, and pundits urge the Fed to lower interest rates and expand bank reserves, they do so in the name of "increasing credit" or "creating investment and jobs." They do not acknowledge the larger issues of inflation, nor do they address the ultimate consequences of such policies.

Likewise, we hear advocates of government regulation extolling the virtues of the regulated economy. For example, they hold up the collapse of Enron as an example of what happens in the absence of regulation, not pointing out that the energy industry is highly regulated. Moreover, Enron's problems did not occur because of its investments in the relatively unregulated area of derivatives, but because of its heavy losses in the regulated sectors of consulting and technology. For that matter, the collapse of numerous savings and loan institutions during the late 1980s occurred in a very heavily regulated industry—but also an industry that had been a favorite haunt of the political classes, which saw S&Ls as cash cows for campaign contributions and other favors.

The regulatory apparatus that now inundates business owners and other professionals with hundreds of thousands of regulations in this country is a product of the Progressive Era. Economic regulation, however, is much older. For example, one of the best-known regulators in history was Jean Baptist Colbert, the finance minister for Louis XIV who regulated the French economy down to the required thickness of threads for textiles. Regulation was not the exception of post-Medieval Europe and England, but the rule, as has been documented by Robert Ekelund and Robert Tollison in their book Politicized Economies.

What is important to remember here is that regulation in those times —while being publicized as something to enhance the "public good" (meaning the political authorities) — was used primarily as a tool to promote politically-favored monopolies and to strangle economic competition. One thing that made the new American colonies favorable places to live was that their business practices were relatively unregulated by government, as opposed to what existed in the Old World.

For about a century after the founding of the United States, business activity faced little or no government regulation, especially compared with the situation in modern times. That began to change during the Progressive Era, a period of time in the late 1800s and early 1900s when the intellectual foundations of law and justice in the United States were turned upside down.

Advocates of Progressivism, which included many intellectuals and journalists of that day, along with politicians such as Theodore Roosevelt, William Jennings Bryan, and Woodrow Wilson, held that the federal system of delegated powers was archaic and out of date for a "modern, progressive" society. Their legal strategy did not only include stripping powers from state and local governments and transferring them to Washington, DC, but they also were successful in convincing members of Congress to give up their own constitutionally-designated powers.

This was done through the crafting of regulatory agencies. The US Constitution gives Congress the power to "regulate" interstate commerce, but the regulatory agencies that Congress created to carry out the increasing number of rules were part of the executive branch of the US government. In other words, Congress, through a legal sleight of hand, redelegated those powers that the Constitution had given Congress, which clearly was a violation of that document.

The first of these agencies was the Interstate Commerce Commission, formed in 1887 to regulate railroads. (This agency set railroad freight and passenger rates, and allocated lines, which turned the nation's once-competitive railroad firms into a vastly regulated cartel.) Other agencies followed such as the Food and Drug Administration and the Federal Trade Commission. By the end of the twentieth century, regulatory agencies dominated the political and economic landscape of this country.

Defenders of the practice of re-delegation (which was routinely approved by the federal courts, which also became stacked with "progressives") argued that the regulatory agencies simply were carrying out the mandate of Congress, which supposedly specified the bounds of regulation in laws that created the agencies or that created new mandates for agencies to follow. Furthermore, it has been argued that there is no law in which regulation of actions can be specific enough to cover every aspect of a certain subject. Regulations, according to this line of argument, must serve the same purpose for civil and criminal law that the Talmud does for the Torah. Regulations do not change the intention of the law, but rather help to spell out its specifics.

That most certainly is not true. Take for example the use of the Civil Rights Act of 1964 as a tool to impose things like racial quotas, despite the fact that the act expressly forbids such quotas. (Sen. Hubert Humphrey, speaking on the US Senate floor in favor of the bill, declared that he would "eat" the paper upon which the law was written if it contained racial quotas.) Seven years later, the US Supreme Court would agree with the US Commission on Civil Rights that the language of that law permitted such quotas.

The executive branch has become a secondary producer of law, its interpreter, as well as its enforcer. The upshot of all this is that government regulations today supposedly operate under the administration of Congress but in reality have become a law unto themselves, with bureaucrats being the nearly-untouchable enforcers.

Take, for example, the numerous abuses of taxpayers by agents from the Internal Revenue Service. As James Bovard painstakingly noted in Feeling Your Pain, IRS agents time and again have acted illegally, yet have faced no consequences, legal or otherwise. The reason is that regulators answer only to themselves or other members of the executive branch, and unless the political heat becomes unbearable, they usually are given a free pass.

This system clearly is unconstitutional—if one holds to the actual language of the US Constitution—yet it is almost universally praised and admired.

This Byzantine and out-of-control system cannot ever be "fixed" by politicians. Furthermore, no US president is going to voluntarily surrender his powers in the way that Congress has done over the past century. Yet, the modern regulatory apparatus is as much a threat to the freedom and well-being of us all as was the destructive system of rules imposed by Colbert upon the hapless French populace.

It is not becoming a law unto itself; it already has reached that stage. The only thing that can be done to end this reign of terror by bureaucrats is to abolish the entire US regulatory system and return to the common law system that served this country so well for so long.

It is just common sense that if we want the economy to grow and we want new, lasting jobs to be created, we must not do things that create obstacles to those goals. So what are we to do to get a handle on our precarious economic situation? Reduce regulations and lift restrictions to encourage business development and to make it easier to do business.

Government can only create government jobs. These jobs are not self-sustaining like private sector jobs but require tax dollars to fund them. More federal jobs means more tax burden on business who will scale back investment as tax burdens increase, thus shifting more economic activity into government hands.

We can't afford government involvement. We need to try something different. Government has already mortgaged our children's future with ballooning debt and is devaluing wealth with inflation.

Right now government intervention works as a kind of morphine to ease the pain; the problem comes if the patient becomes addicted, as it happened after the Great Depression and World War II. The main cause of socialism has been always the Defense Department.

Freedom, among other things, means freedom of choice. Freedom cannot mean the imposition of government taxes or regulatory measures, no matter what form of government produces them. Freedom cannot mean centralized or collectivized controls backed up by the force of the State.

8 "SACRIFICING A LITTLE LIBERTY FOR SECURITY NEVER HURT ANYONE."

When the endless attacks on personal liberty become undeniable, some statists will fall back on this one. Yeah sure the state intrudes on your lives but it's all for your protection and hey! Freedom's overrated anyway!

This is another tragic case of claiming to solve a problem when in fact you have only deferred it. Sure, if against all odds you managed to completely purge all guns from a society so that only the police and military have them, yeah you probably are pretty safe from being shot by a criminal.

One problem: What's going to protect you from the police and the military should power go to their heads? They are but mere mortals after all, and you know what they say about absolute power corrupting absolutely.

This argument is based on the flawed idea that safety and freedom work at cross purposes. The strength of one means the weakness of the other but nothing could be further from the truth. The truth is they go hand in hand. Freedom is a very friendly person that way.

You see, when people are free, they will naturally migrate towards whatever endeavors they personally feel comfortable with thus whatever proves itself the safest will naturally thrive while undue risk fades away. To instead trust our safety to one elite and unaccountable group is quite literally putting all of one's eggs in one very flimsy basket which is anything but safe. This is why Ben Franklin warned us that those who sacrifice freedom for safety deserve neither, because you sure as hell won't get either one in the end.

To assert a tension or tradeoff between "liberty" and "security" is inevitably subjective. It would be no less objective, nor any more "Orwellian," to assert that liberty and security are one -- that liberty exists only where there is security. Of course, such an assertion begs the definition of "security," but it's always been up to a body politic to define both that term and "liberty" to the satisfaction of its members.

Indeed, many feel that perpetual insecurity deprives them of liberty, while many others fear that statism makes their liberty insecure. It's probably a natural feeling in either case

Enemies can be domestic as well as foreign, and liberty also provides us the greatest security against domestic enemies, people who would subvert our Constitution and arrogate power to themselves illegitimately. Our civil liberties prevent the peaceful accumulation of power that can be turned despotic. This is true most obviously of the liberties in the Bill of Rights, such as the Second and Tenth Amendments, the Fourth, Sixth, and Eighth

Amendments, and the First Amendment. These liberties—if we stick up for them vigorously enough—prevent the national government from legislating "thought crimes," and arresting people without charges, torturing confessions out of the innocent, or usurping the powers that were supposed to be exercised closer to home.

Liberty promotes self-reliance and discourages the kind of dependency that can too easily be exploited for political control.

Federal money has long been used to coerce states into adopting policies dreamed up in Washington, no matter how ill-suited those policies are to the state's actual circumstances. (Remember when the speed limit was 55 MPH across the country, no matter if you were in downtown Los Angeles or in the badlands of Nevada) Sometimes federal mandates do not fit the needs of every locality. Many public and private organizations are coerced by the prospect of losing federal subsidies. Using coercion in this way, the federal government could potentially exercise too much power over them because of this method of influence it has on these organizations. Educational institutions are similarly coerced by the prospect of losing federal grant money. And more recently, coercive federal health care regulations have placed private schools and hospitals in the uncomfortable position of having to choose between their deeply and sincerely held religious beliefs and the ability to continue serving the poor through their charitable institutions. The general rule is clear: When people pay to support the government, the people are in charge; when government pays to support the people, the politicians hold too many trump cards.

Liberty promotes sound foreign policy. Ron Paul has told us all about the virtues of a non-interventionist foreign policy, but I would like to add that we are much more likely to catch ourselves overreaching abroad if we are still sensitive to government overreaching at home. Statist economic policies and imperialist foreign policies both presuppose that government planning is superior to individual liberty. That presupposition is poison, and we must purge ourselves of it.

On a primal level, we all desire to be secure. Men and women each tend to view security in a different way. Perhaps the desire for security explains why many women more easily tend to embrace statism. Many women tend to see statism as a social function rather than political, while most men are more likely to view statism as a political process instead of a social. Thus, many women embrace statism because they tend to see that process providing a sense of security.

Many men today still accept the traditional role of provider and protector. Providing and protecting is challenging enough without having to engage the political conflicts and illusions of wealth redistribution. Thus, men tend to recognize coerced political systems as legalized theft under the color of law. Possibly, a woman initially does not tend to see wealth redistribution as theft because of her social nature and focus to provide security for her home.

Politics is merely a process of coercively transferring wealth from one class of people to another. By understanding this truth, the woman who travels this journey eventually realizes that political processes will do more to destroy than help her sense of security. Thus, when a woman fully understands the theft that occurs through political systems she accurately sees the security of her home threatened.

Freedom *from* Government: Statist Delusions

When a man illustrates the concept of coerced wealth redistribution, he must explain those differences from the perspective of how free association and voluntary exchange are more beneficial and reciprocating toward providing and maintaining a woman's desire for security. Men must be prepared to show women how statism discourages voluntary sharing and inhibits rather than encourages everyone from getting along. Through that educational process a man always must remember that the moment a woman perceives the security of her home being threatened, she will bail out of any further discussion.

This also applies to single women. Regardless of their own physical abilities, to one degree or another single women more than likely live in a somewhat heightened state of fear and uncertainty. They fear attack from predators of one form or another. Thus, men need to be aware of a woman's general desire for security and explain how a single woman would find stronger security in a world void of coercive political systems.

What constitutional liberties will they not crush as the statists' national security state continually expands to fit a bunch of bureaucrats' cookie-cutter idea of "safety"?

We all need to understand our desire for security from a different perspective — a perspective never provided to us by people working in the statist educational system, politics, or general media. Provide the security one seeks and they will be more inclined to listen to arguments opposing statism.

Fear of insecurity, and responsibility. Emotions have been overriding logic and reason, those in power are capitalizing on emotions not truth. The battle is between those who cherish security but don't want to accept the responsibility for that security. Large segments of our population want to assign the responsibility for their security to the government. They don't want to be personally accountable for mitigating danger and risk to which they are exposed. They are more than willing to allow the government the power to use force to restrict the liberty of others so that they can "feel" secure. The problem is that the government isn't actually accountable for providing any individual with security.

Another part of our society still values liberty, and are more than willing to accept the fact that to have liberty you must accept the responsibility to provide your own security. To have freedom is not free, because independence means that you are not dependent upon the government. The more things that you depend upon the government to provide, the more control of your actions you must grant the government.

To have Liberty you must accept and embrace the fact that the government has no legal or moral authority to provide you individually with security. The government is not accountable for, nor responsible for providing you with security. You accept the risk that you must provide your own food, clothing, shelter, healthcare, happiness, and protection. In a free society the government's sole responsibility is to protect you're right to pursue those things, not grant you those things. The reason is that for the government to provide you with security it must be allowed and have the power to control. You can't be responsible to mitigate risks and provide safety if you don't have control. So if you want more security you must grant control to the entity accountable for providing that security. This is why the Supreme Court has consistently ruled that the police are not responsible to protect any individual. Since the police cannot control the movement, actions, etc. of individuals, they are not accountable for any individual's security. The responsibility for security lies with whomever controls the actions, movement, etc. for an individual. Hence parents are responsible to their children for providing security, they also have control of those children.

Whoever is in control is responsible; period. Public schools are a prime example. Public schools exercise *in loco parentis*. The term *in loco parentis*, is Latin for "*in the place of a parent*" and refers to the legal responsibility of a person or organization to take on some of the functions and responsibilities of a parent. This means that the school has the right to act as a parent while children are at school. This gives them the legal authority to have much more control over students than the government normally has over individuals. They have *in loco parentis* because they also have the legal and moral responsibility to provide security for their students. That's why, within reasonable bounds, a school has the right to limit student behavior in schools even if that same behavior out of the school is totally legal. Hence a school can limit students from wearing gang colors while at school but not when those same students are out of school. So with responsibility comes control, and you can't be responsible for what you don't control.

Large parts of our society don't want to be responsible for their own security so are willing to give control to the government in exchange for security. They want the emotional feeling that security provides, even if it's illusionary. This is a huge conflict with those who value Liberty over Security. Those who want to control their own lives, and determine their own destiny are not willing to give control to anybody, especially the state.

In the Newtown catastrophe in 2012, those responsible for the security of the students, the government school, who were granted large amounts control via *in loco parentis*, failed. The government school is responsible for the safety of the children in their care. The government exercised control by creating laws and rules that said nobody is allowed to have the tools to defend themselves or others at this government facility, they made it a "gun-free zone." The government was responsible for providing freedom from danger. The government not only took that responsibility, but denied others the right to exercise that responsibility. Now those in Washington want that control, but they won't subject their children to the same risks as the "public" school children in Newtown. Obama, most of congress and the senate don't send their kids to "public" schools where the government is in control of security. They instead send their kids to private schools, with armed personnel specifically assigned to provide security, usually by having firearms of the type they want to deny every other citizen from having. They want and have taken responsibility for the security of their children, but don't want the general public to have the same security. They think that their ability to hire others to be that security is of greater value than poorer people taking individual personal responsibility is morally superior. That the rich ruling elite are saying, "If you can't afford to pay somebody to provide you with armed security, you aren't entitled to armed security."

Why is the government plainly using the example of Newtown, where they failed in their responsibility to provide students with security, as an excuse to take away citizens' rights to the tools that allow them to effectively provide for their own security? Why is hiring armed people to protect you and your children morally superior to arming yourself to protect you and your children?

The ruling elite have said, because of our greater wealth and position, we deserve and will have control over the security of ourselves and our children, but you the masses cannot have control of your own security. They are clearly saying Liberty for me, but not for thee. They simply prey on the fears of those who don't want or are afraid to assume personal responsibility. Many of the masses have proven more than willing to give the ruling elite control. Those afraid of having to be responsible for themselves, want a "right" to feel safe and secure, even if that means taking away the natural rights of others. This is a battle between those who don't want responsibility for their own security, and those who want liberty.

If it truly was about security of children then they would be up in arms about 2012's five-hundred deaths of school age children and thousands of injuries in Chicago alone. The truth is the government and press is only in an uproar over Newtown because it was white kids killed; in Chicago the situation is black kids killed by other blacks so they just don't care. Black on black violent crime is so common the press rarely cover it. The government has created laws that target young black males, arrested them, convict them, and imprison them at massive rates, so they can deny them their second amendment (and other) rights. The liberal press's and statist politicians' cries concerning the massacre at Newtown are racist, they don't care and don't say anything concerning massive deaths of black people, they only care and want action because Newtown was white kids being killed. In 2012 Chicago had the equivalent of a Newtown child massacre every two weeks, it also has the strictest gun laws in the nation, the press and politicians know this. They aren't dumb. They know more gun laws are not the answer, but more gun laws are a way to increase state control. Until and unless they make the government legally responsible for the security of individuals, they have no moral authority to take control of the tools of providing effective security. The government wants the control but not the responsibility for security. If you can't see that you are blind.

The fact is if you are against the restrictions on government as instituted in the Bill of Rights, you are in favor of oppression; period. Letting the state deny an individual the control of their own security without the state accepting the legal and moral responsibility for an individual's security, is in fact supporting statist tyranny. Fighting tyranny of the state is the reason the people included the severe restriction on the government known as the Second Amendment. Not because we have a tyrannical state, but because history has shown, repeatedly, that states can and do become tyrannical and an armed people have the means of fighting a tyrannical state.

If the fact that your neighbor owns or might own an AR-15, and a few other guns scares you, move. Your fear doesn't negate your neighbor's rights; you have no right to not be afraid any more than you have a right to feel happy, sad, or mad, your feelings are not rights, and fear is just that, an emotion. Until and unless you can prove your neighbor has committed a felony or is mentally unfit, in a court of law, where he can call witnesses, cross examine, and defend himself, you have no right to control how he chooses to be responsible for his own security.

The courts have consistently ruled against the government exercising "prior restraint." They have also consistently ruled that neither the police nor the state have a legal or moral responsibility to provide any individual with security. When thinking of security ask yourself, who is legally and morally

Freedom *from* Government: Statist Delusions

responsible to provide that security and why? If you think it's the government you are in the wrong country and should consider moving to another, like China, where the government clearly takes the legal and moral responsibility for its citizens, along with control of where they work, what they earn, what they receive, what they say, what they read, etc.

9 "TAXES ARE FEES FOR SERVICES."

So if taxes are fees for services, then why is it a percentage of your income, and not apportioned according to services you use? Theoretically it's not like Bill Gates is getting more roads, courts, police or other services than I am so why does he pay more than me? That really doesn't make any sense. If taxes were fees for services, wouldn't you pay them based on the amount of services you use, or have used? And since a service cannot be forced on you without your permission or knowledge the service should not also be able to demand whatever price they want with no prior agreement. Can I mow your lawn while you're sleeping and leave a bill demanding a hundred dollars for the work? There is no court in the world would take that seriously for even a second and yet for some an inexplicable reason it's considered completely moral and sane when the state does it. Demanding a percentage of one's income is far more consistent with the behavior of the mafia than any legitimate business

When the mafia demands 10% of your income or else, it's called racketeering; when the government demands 40% of your income or else, it's called taxation and is somehow now something totally different. And my only question is *how*? The statist will usually reply, "The government uses that money to help people! It's not stealing!"

Why does the question of whose property it is never come up? Does government own a share of everyone's productivity and this entire plot of land and we are just serfs working it? Did the government homestead or voluntarily buy every plot of land or is my home property which I built or bought voluntarily. What give other people the right to tell others what to do with one's own property? These are just double standards because I wouldn't be surprised if a statist also said that government has consent of the people. How can it if the people who don't consent don't count? It's very easy to have government be based on consent if you don't account for those who do not consent.

Maybe I could go rob a bank, and then donate a fair chunk of it to an orphanage. Then when I'm arrested I could just argue in court that I didn't steal the money because I donated the majority of it to a good cause and see how far that argument goes in court!

Even if taxation was money legitimately owed to the state, how exactly does that justify threats of violence for non-payment? When you borrow from a credit card company and don't pay it back, what happens? They send your name to collections and you get your credit rating shot. When you borrow from the mafia and don't pay it back, what happens? They send armed men to your house. Which one sounds more like what the state does?

I am among the tens of millions of Americans who don't file tax returns or voluntarily pay taxes, I do not support the government anymore, and as such I have withdrawn all the support for it that I can.

Paying taxes and voting are both similar in that they are activities that demand involvement with a coercive and violent institution known as government. Government exercises a monopoly of legal control over a certain geographic area. This encompasses coercive and violent monopolization of the major services that it provides us. To fund these services, the government unilaterally imposes a compulsory levy upon us. These "taxes" are not based on the amount of service the government provides us, nor upon our request for them. The government does not offer us the opportunity to opt-out of a particular service, or shop elsewhere for it, or to negotiate the price. It doesn't care if we didn't want the service, didn't use all that was offered, or simply refused it altogether. The government declares it a crime if we refuse to pay all or part of what it has determined to be "our share." It attempts to punish this refusal by making us serve time in jail or confiscating some of our property, or both.

So, the main reason why I refuse to pay income taxes is that I don't want to give my sanction to the government. I, for one, do not consent to our particular government, nor do I want to support any coercive or violent institution. I object on principle, to the forced collection of taxes because taxes are a euphemism for stealing. We all know what stealing is; when I say stealing, I mean taking another person's property without their voluntary consent. Stealing is not an activity that leads to social harmony or prosperity. Stealing is anti-life. It is not an activity that can be universalized. If it were collectively morally acceptable to steal, the result would likely be death and destruction for all. Furthermore, "stealing" or "taxation" is wasteful. Everyone (even statists) can agree that government money is commonly spent unwisely, wastefully, and on at least some projects which would never be voluntarily supported by some taxpayers. Even if the government spending were not wasteful, or used for some immoral purpose I would still object strenuously because taxes are theft to begin with. In other words, what I really object to is the coercive means that are used by government, regardless of how efficiently the money is spent or what it is spent on. I do not want it said about me that I cooperated with, or supported the actions of the government as long as it uses violence and immorality to achieve its ends.

Similarly, I refuse to participate in the electoral process (I simply refuse to register to vote) because I do not want it ever said that I supported the state. When you play a game, you agree to abide by the rules and accept the outcome. Well, I simply refuse to play, and in clear conscience can say that I am not bound by the outcome. Furthermore, there are many reprehensible activities taken by the government (you can choose your own example) which I do not wish to support. Governments need legitimacy, and one of the major means of establishing legitimacy is to claim that the voters support the government. Just imagine if everyone refused to vote and pay taxes. Government would shrivel up. But, before that happened legislators at every level would probably pass laws that would make voting compulsory. This has already happened in some countries.

In other words, in refusing to "register" to pay taxes, I am going back to the old, traditional standards of morality, ethics, common law, and common sense. I am refusing to act in a way that produces or contributes to evil.

The Encyclopedia Britannica defines taxation as "that part of the revenues of a state which is obtained by the compulsory dues and charges upon its subjects." That is about as concise and accurate as a definition can be; it leaves no room for argument as to what taxation is. In that statement of fact the word "compulsory" looms large, simply because of its ethical content. The quick reaction is to question the "right" of the State to this use of power. What sanction, in morals, does the State use to justify the taking of property? Is its claim and exercise of sovereignty sufficient unto itself? Are we all subjects of the state by default?

On this question of morality there are two positions, and never the twain will meet. Those who hold that political institutions stem from "the social contract," thus enjoying vicarious divine right, including those who pronounce the State the keystone of social assimilations, can find no quarrel with taxation per se; the State's taking of property is justified by its existence or its inherent authority.

On the other hand, those who hold to the authority of the individual, whose very existence is his claim to inalienable rights, lean to the position that in the compulsory collection of dues and charges the State is merely exercising power, without regard to morals.

The inquiry into taxation begins with the first of these positions. It is as biased as would be an inquiry starting with the similarly unverifiable proposition that the State is either a natural or a socially necessary institution. Complete fairness is excluded when an ethical suggestion is the major premise of an argument; and a rational discussion of the nature of taxation cannot ignore values.

If we assume that the individual has an indisputable right to life, we must concede that he has a similar right to the enjoyment of the products of his labor. This we call a property right. The absolute right to property follows from the original right to life because one without the other is meaningless; the means to life must be identified with life itself. If the State has a foregoing right to the products of one's labor, the individual does not truly have a complete right to his life because he indebted to the state for a percentage of his earnings. Time was expended by the individual in the form of labor, so essentially the state is assuming that it is entitled to a percentage of one's life. Aside from the fact that no such prior right can be established, except by declaring the State the author of all rights, our inclination (as shown in the effort to avoid paying taxes) is to reject this concept of priority. Our instinct is against it. We object to the taking of our property by organized society just as we do when a single unit of society commits the act. In the latter case we unhesitatingly call the act robbery. It is not the law which in the first instance defines robbery, it is an ethical principle, and the law may not supersede morals. If by the necessity of living we acquiesce to the force of law, if by long custom we lose sight of the immorality, has the principle been obliterated? Robbery is robbery, and no amount of words can make it anything else.

A historical study of taxation leads inevitably to loot, tribute, and ransom the profitable fruits of conquest. The barons who put up toll-gates along the Rhine were tax-gatherers. So were the gangs who "protected," for a forced fee, the caravans going to market. The conquering Romans introduced the idea that what they collected from subject peoples was merely just payment for maintaining "law and order." For a long time the Norman conquerors collected catch-as-catch-can tribute from the English, but when by natural processes and the fusion of the two peoples resulted in a nation, the collections were regularized in custom and law and were called taxes. It took centuries to obliterate the idea that these exactions served but to keep a privileged class in comfort and to finance their domestic wars; in fact, that purpose was never denied or obscured until constitutionalism diffused political power.

As to method of collection, taxation falls into two categories, direct and indirect. Indirect taxes are so called because they reach the state by way of private collectors, while direct taxes arrive without detour. The former levies are attached to goods and services before they reach the consumer, while the latter are mainly demands upon accumulations of wealth.

It will be seen that indirect taxation is a permission-to-live price. You cannot find in the marketplace a single satisfaction to which a number of these taxes are not attached, hidden in the price, and you are under compulsion either to pay them or go without; since going without amounts to depriving yourself of the meaning of life, or even of life itself, you end up paying the tax. The inevitability of this charge on existence is expressed in the popular association of death and taxes. And it is this very characteristic that commends indirect taxation to the state, so that when you examine the prices of things you live by, you are astounded by the disproportion between the cost of production and the charge for permission to buy. Somebody has put the number of taxes carried by a loaf of bread at over one hundred; obviously, some are not ascertainable, for it would be impossible to allocate to each loaf its share of taxes on the broom used in the bakery, on the axle-grease used on the delivery wagon. Whiskey is perhaps the most notorious example of the way products have been transmuted from satisfactions into tax-gatherers. The manufacturing cost of a gallon of whiskey, for which the consumer pays around twenty dollars, is less than a dollar; the spread is partly accounted for in the costs of distribution, but most of the money which passes over the counter goes to maintain city, county, state and national officials.

The dissent and cry over the cost of living would make more sense if it were directed at taxation, the largest single item in the cost. It should be noted too that though the cost-of-living problem affects mainly the poor, yet it is on this segment of society that the incidence of indirect taxation falls most heavily. This is necessarily so; since those in the lower earning brackets constitute the major portion of society they must account for the greatest share of consumption, and therefore for the greatest share of taxation. The state recognizes this fact in levying on goods of widest use. A tax on salt, no matter how small comparatively, yields much more than a tax on diamonds, and is of greater significance socially and economically.

It is not the size of the yield, nor the certainty of collection, which gives indirect taxation preeminence in the State's scheme of appropriation. Its most commendable quality is that of being surreptitious. It is taking, so to speak, while the victim is not looking. Those who strain themselves to give taxation a moral character are under obligation to explain the State's preoccupation with hiding taxes in the price of goods. Is there a confession of guilt in that? In recent years, in its search for additional revenue, the State has been tinkering with a sales tax, an outright and unequivocal permission-to-live price; wiser statesmen have opposed this measure on the ground of political expediency. Why? If the State serves a good purpose the producers will hardly object to paying its keep.

Merely as a matter of method, not with deliberate in-tent, indirect taxation yields a profit of proportions to private collectors, and for this reason opposition to the levies could hardly be expected from that corner. When the tax is paid in advance of the sale it becomes an element of cost which must be added to all other costs in computing price. As the expected profit is a percentage of the total outlay, it will be seen that the tax itself becomes a source of gain. Where the merchandise must pass through the hands of several processors and distributors, the profits pyramided on the tax can run up to as much as, if not more than, the amount collected by the State. The consumer pays the tax plus the compounded profits. Particularly notorious in this regard are customs duties. Follow an importation of raw silk, from importer to cleaner, to spinner, to weaver, to finisher, to manufacturer, to wholesaler, to retailer, each one adding his markup to the price paid his predecessor, and you will see that in the price the consumer pays for her gown there is much more than the tariff schedule demands. This fact alone helps to make merchants and manufacturers indifferent to the evils of protection.

Tacit support for indirect taxation arises from another by-product. Where a considerable outlay in taxes is a prerequisite for engaging in a business, large accumulations of capital have a distinct competitive advantage, and these capitalists could hardly be expected to advocate a lowering of the taxes. Any farmer can make whiskey, and many of them do; but the necessary investment in revenue stamps and various license fees makes the opening of a distillery and the organizing of distributive agencies a business only for large capital. Taxation has forced the locally-owned and good-natured brewer to yield to the corporate brewery or distillery that has enough financial backing to pay all the licensing fees and taxes. Likewise, the manufacture of cigarettes is concentrated in the hands of a few giant corporations by the help of our tax system; nearly three-quarters of the retail price of a package of cigarettes represents an outlay in taxes. It would be strange indeed if these interests were to voice opposition to such indirect taxes (which they never do) and the uninformed, inarticulate and unorganized consumer is forced to pay the higher price resulting from limited competition.

Direct taxes differ from indirect taxes not only in the manner of collection but also in the more important fact that they cannot be passed on; those who pay them cannot demand reimbursement from others. Mainly direct taxation falls on incomes and accumulations rather than on goods in the course of exchange. You are taxed on what you have earned, not on something you buy Taxed on the proceeds of enterprise or the returns from services already rendered, not on anticipated revenue. Hence there is no way of shifting the burden. The payer has no recourse.

The clear cut direct taxes are those levied on incomes, inheritances, gifts, land values. It can be noted that such misappropriations lend themselves to more propaganda, and find support in the envy of the incompetent, the bitterness of poverty, and the sense of injustice which our monopoly economy engenders. Direct taxation has been advocated since colonial times (along with universal suffrage), as the necessary implementation of democracy, as the essential instrument of "leveling." The opposition of the rich to direct taxation added virulence to the reformers who plugged for it. In normal times the State is unable to overcome this articulate and resourceful opposition. But, when war or the need of improving mass poverty strains the purse of the state to the limit, and further in-direct impositions are impossible or threaten social unrest, the opposition must give way. The state never relinquishes entirely the sanctions it acquires during an "emergency," and so, after a series of wars and depressions direct taxation became a fixture of our fiscal policy, and those upon whom it falls must content themselves to whittling down the levies or trying to transfer them from shoulder to shoulder.

Even as it was predicted, during the debates on the income tax in the early part of the century, it was impossible for the State to contain itself once this instrument of getting additional revenue was put into its hands. Income is income whether it stems from dividends, bootlegging operations, gambling profits or plain wages. As the expenses of the state mount, and they always do, legal inhibitions and considerations of justice or mercy are swept aside, and the state dips its hands into every pocket. These, by the way, make evident utter immorality of political power. Social security taxation is nothing but a tax on wages, in its entirety, and was deliberately and maliciously misnamed. Even the part which is "contributed" by the employer is ultimately paid by the worker in the price of the goods he consumes, for it is obvious that this part is merely a cost of operation and is passed on, with a mark-up. The revenue from social security taxes is not set aside for the payment of social "benefits," but is thrown into the general tax fund, subject to any appropriation, and when an old-age pittance is ultimately allowed it is paid out of the then current tax collections. It is in no way comparable to insurance, by which fiction it made its way into our fiscal policy, but it is a direct tax on wages.

There are more people in the low income brackets than in the high brackets; there are more small donations than large ones. Therefore, in the aggregate, those least able to meet the burden of luxury taxes bear the brunt of them. The attempt to offset this inequity by a system of graduations is unreal. Even a small tax on an income of one thousand dollars a year will cause the payer some hardship, while a fifty percent tax on fifty thousand dollars leaves something to live on comfortably. There is a vast difference between doing without a new automobile and wearing a patched-up pair of pants to do more service. It should be remembered, too, that the worker's income is almost always confined to wages, which are a matter of record. While large incomes are mainly derived from business or gambling operations, and are not so easily ascertainable. Whether it is from intent to avoid paying the full tax, or from the necessary legal ambiguities which make the exact amount a matter of conjecture or bookkeeping, those with large incomes are favored. It is the poor who are soaked most heavily by income and other direct taxes.

Taxes also discourage production. Man works to satisfy his desires, not to support the state. When the results of his labors are taken from him, whether by thieves or organized society, his inclination is to limit his production to the amount he can keep and enjoy. During the war, when the payroll deduction was introduced, workers got to figuring their "take home" pay, and to laying off when this net, after taxes, showed no increase comparable to the extra work it would cost; leisure is also a satisfaction. A prize fighter refuses another lucrative engagement because the additional revenue would bring his income for the year into a higher tax bracket. In like manner, every business man must take into consideration, when weighing the risk and the possibility of profit in a new enterprise, the certainty of a tax offset in the event of success, and too often he is discouraged from going ahead. In all the data on national progress the items that can never be reported are: the volume of business choked off by income taxes, and the size of capital accumulations aborted by inheritance taxes.

While we are on the subject of discouragement of production by taxation, we should not overlook the greater weight of indirect taxes, even though it is not so obvious. The production level of a nation is determined by the purchasing power of its people. It is to this extent that power is absorbed by levies, to the extent that it brings down the production level. It is thoroughly indecent to maintain that what the state collects it spends, and that therefore there is no lowering of total purchasing power. Thieves also spend their loot, with much more abandon than the rightful owners would have spent it, and on the basis of spending one could make out a case for the social value of thievery. It is production, not spending, that begets production. It is only by the feeding of marketable contributions into the general fund of wealth that the gears of industry are sped up. Inversely, every deduction from this general fund of wealth slows down industry, and every levy on savings discourages the accumulation of capital. Why work when there is nothing in it? Why go into business to support politicians?

In principle, as the framers of the Constitution realized, the direct tax is most vicious, for it directly denies the sanctity of private property. By its very existence the indirect tax is an under-handed slur to the recognition of the right of the individual to his earnings. The state sneaks up on the owner so to speak, and takes what it needs on the grounds of necessity and authority. All the while in reality it does not even have the authority to question the right of the owner to his goods. The direct tax, however, boldly and unashamedly proclaims the prior right of the state to all property. Private ownership becomes a temporary and revocable tenancy. The Jeffersonian ideal of inalienable rights is thus liquidated, and substituted for it is the Marxist concept of state supremacy. It is by this fiscal policy, rather than by violent revolution, or by an appeal to reason, or by popular education, or by way of any foreseeable forces, that the substance of Socialism is realized. Notice how the centralization hoped for by Alexander Hamilton has been achieved since the advent of the federal income tax, how the contemplated union of independent commonwealths is effectively dissolved. The commonwealths are reduced to parish status, the individual no longer is a citizen of his community but is a subject of the federal government.

A basic immorality becomes the center of a vortex of immoralities. When the state invades the right of the individual to the products of his labors it appropriates an authority which is contrary to the nature of things and therefore establishes an unethical pattern of behavior, for itself and those upon whom its authority is exerted. Thus, the income tax has made the State a partner in the proceeds of crime; the law cannot distinguish between incomes derived from production and incomes derived from robbery; it has no concern with the source. Likewise, this denial of ownership arouses a resentment which breaks out into perjury and dishonesty. Men who in their personal affairs would hardly think of such methods, or who would be socially ostracized for practicing them, are proud of, and are complimented for, evasion of the income tax laws; it is considered proper to engage the shrewdest minds for that purpose. More degrading even is the encouragement by bribes of mutual spying. No other single measure in the history of our country has caused a comparable disregard of principle in public affairs, or has had such a deteriorating effect on morals.

To make its way into the good will of its victims, taxation has surrounded itself with doctrines of justification. No law which lacks public approval or acquiescence is enforceable, and to gain such support it must address itself to our sense of correctness. This is particularly necessary for statutes authorizing the taking of private property.

Taxation for social services hints at an equitable trade. It suggests a quid pro quo, a relationship of justice. But, the essential condition of trade, that it be carried on willingly, is absent from taxation; it's very use of compulsion removes taxation from the field of commerce and puts it squarely into the field of politics. Taxes cannot be compared to dues paid to a voluntary organization for such services as one expects from membership, because the choice of withdrawal does not exist. In refusing to trade one may deny oneself a profit, but the only alternative to paying taxes is jail. The suggestion of equity in taxation is spurious. If we get anything for the taxes we pay it is not because we want it; it is forced on us.

In respect to social services a community may be compared to a large office building in which the occupants, carrying on widely differing businesses, make use of common conveniences, such as elevator transportation, cleaning, heating, and so on. The more tenants in the building, the more dependent are they all on these overall specializations, and at a pro rata fee the operators of the building supply them; the fee is included in the room rent. Each of the tenants is enabled to carry on his business more efficiently because he is relieved of his share of the overall duties.

Just so are the citizens of a community better able to carry on their several occupations because the streets are maintained, the fire department is on guard, the police department provides protection to life and property. When a society is organizing, as in a frontier town, the need for these overall services is met by volunteer labor. The road is kept open by its users, there is a volunteer fire department, the respected elder performs the services of a judge. As the town grows these extra-curricular jobs become too onerous and too complicated for volunteers, whose private affairs must suffer by the increasing demands, and the necessity of hiring specialists arises. To meet the expense, it is claimed, compulsory taxation must be resorted to, and the question is, why must the residents be compelled to pay for being relieved of work which they formerly performed willingly? Why is coercion a correlative of taxation?

It is not true that the services would be impossible without taxation; that assertion is denied by the fact that the services appear before taxes are introduced. The services come because there is need for them. Because there is need for them they are paid for, in the beginning, with labor and, in a few instances, with voluntary contributions of goods and money; the trade is without compulsion and therefore equitable. Only when political power takes over the management of these services does the compulsory tax appear. It is not the cost of the services which calls for taxation, it is the cost of maintaining political power.

So, if I approach you on the street and demand money from you would you give it to me? What if I threatened you with a gun? Would it be right for me to insist you give me the money from your wallet? What if I only wanted one third of the money in your wallet? What if I promised you protection and other services in return for the money? Would you consider this theft? I imagine you would. It would be not only mugging, but robbery, and extortion. And you would be right in that assessment.

What if I stopped you on the street and had 10 people agreeing that you should give me the money? Would it still be theft? Of course it would. How about 100 people? 1,000? 10,000? 1,000,000? At what point does it no longer qualify as theft, robbery or extortion? If your answer is "never" then you're not only a rational human being, but you also agree that taxes are theft, though you may not have realized it.

Because that's exactly what the government has done. They've gathered a large group of people together to assert that they have the right to take one-third (or more) of your money and that you have no choice in the matter. Should you resist, they will shoot you. Don't believe me? Then it's time for another example.

If you stop paying property taxes what do you think is going to happen? The government will send you letter after letter demanding "their" money. They may even make a few phone calls or send some bureaucrat by your house to try and collect. If you continue to refuse to hand over your hard earned money they'll eventually send a police officer, sheriff or other law enforcement officer to your house to evict you.

Notice that gun on the law enforcement officer's hip? It's there for a reason. Because if you refuse to leave the property that you paid for with money that you worked for, and still refuse to hand over a share of that hard earned money to the state, then the law enforcement officer is going to try to handcuff you and drag you off of your property. if you continue to resist he's going to pull that gun and point it at you. If you still refuse to pay their extortion (aka taxes) and still refuse to abandon your little part of the American dream, then the police officers will shoot you. That's what the gun is there for.

The only difference between a mugger in a dark alley and a law enforcement officer is the amount of money they demand from you (the government wants far more than the mugger) and the number of people backing them up.

Slavery is wrong. Taxation is a form of slavery. Therefore taxation is wrong.

Slavery is wrong. A slave is a person who is the property of another or others, such that whatever the slave produces can be taken by force or the threat of force. The slave has no right of self-ownership, and those who exercise dominion over the slave always have the legal right to use coercion against him, but certainly have no natural right to do so. He who takes the life, liberty, or property of another without that other's consent is stealing; and as the early abolitionist described it, man-stealing is just as wrong, if not worse, than property-stealing, because human beings hold a higher rank in existence than inert property matter.

Taxation is a form of slavery. A tax is a compulsory levy on a person subject to the jurisdiction of a government. Anyone who is taxed is a slave because his or her earnings and property are forcibly taken to support the State. Most individuals do not consent to taxation. Historically, the Romance languages, such as French, Spanish, and Italian, have tried to make the tax-payer "feel good" by euphemistically calling him a "contributor".

"Customers" is the term that our own Internal Revenue Service uses to identify those from whom it extracts payments, using threats of force or actual force in some instances.

Therefore taxation is wrong. As Auberon Herbert pointed out decades before the passage of the 16th Amendment to the U.S. Constitution (on the basis of which Congress legislated a federal income tax): "truth and consistency demand that if the State may forcibly take one dollar "out of what a man owns, it may take what it likes up to the last dollar ... Once admit the right of the [S]tate to take, and the [S]tate becomes the real owner of all property." To those who wish to debate this point, I only ask: where in the federal Constitution is there any limitation on the amount that Congress may try to take from us?"

But, as Charles Adams, one historian of taxation has observed: "without revenue, governments would collapse, society as we know it would disappear, and chaos would follow."

True: coercive political governments which depend on violence to sustain themselves with police and armed force would disappear. Yes, society as we know it today in the United States would change.

But would chaos follow? Not necessarily. If the opponents of taxation used revolutionary violence to abolish the State, then there would undoubtedly be some who would fight for the re-establishment of taxation But if taxation were to be abandoned as a result of a shift in public opinion and understanding, then, in the words of Murray Rothbard, we would simply achieve a peaceful "society without a state." As Thomas Paine explained centuries ago: A "[g]reat part of that order which reigns among mankind is not the effect of Government. It has its origins in the principles of society and the natural constitution of man. It existed prior to Government, and would exist if the formality of Government" no longer existed.

All history attests to the fact that if a service supplied by government is truly wanted, a voluntary way will be found to provide it. It may cost some people more than when the government supplied it; but the point is that if a true demand exists, some entrepreneur or some group of individuals will associate cooperatively to provide it. Any number of examples can be used to illustrate this point: Did religion disappear when churches lost their government support? Did people go without coined money when there were no government mints? Did people go shoeless because there were no government factories to produce footwear?

Does our governmentally-directed society based on coercive taxation really work all that well? If we were to start out de novo would we actually entrust all our protective and defensive services to the members of one organization, and empower them to collect their revenues at the point of a gun? What kind of service could we expect from a monopoly that had no competition and a guaranteed income? Who would protect us from our guardians if they turned corrupt? Who would guard the guardians? Voluntary, consensual arrangements are always more flexible and less predictable than those imposed by coercive governments, which always perceive change as a threat to their dominance and sovereignty.

Government taxation is a coercive activity that introduces force and violence into otherwise peaceful relationships. That is our primary reason for opposing taxation. It pits one man against another; one group against another group; upsets the natural market incentives that produce the greatest benefits for all. We believe it is morally proper that a man keep the product of his labor; that he not be enslaved. If it is wrong for a slave owner to enslave a single person, then it is wrong for a group of individuals to do so. Majority rule cannot legitimize slavery or taxation.

Conscientious objectors to taxation recognize that some goods and services are essential to human survival, but also realize they need not be provided by the government on a coercive basis. What we oppose is the coercion involved in collecting taxes. We oppose the means and take the position that the ends never justify the means. Our opposition to taxation doesn't concern itself with whether too much money is being collected, or whether that money is being spent wastefully. Rather, the focus is on the fact that any amount of money forcefully collected is stealing. It is no more proper for government agents to seize property than it is for you to rob your neighbor at gunpoint, even if you spend the money on something that you think will benefit your neighbor.

If some in our society think that certain government services are necessary, then let them collect the revenues to support those services in a voluntary fashion. We who oppose taxation may or may not support their efforts. It would soon be revealed which services are sufficiently desired. And if the people collecting the money to support these services do not, in their judgment, collect enough, then let them dig into their own pockets to make up the deficiency or do without. They do not have the right to spend other people's money.

Taxation is nothing but a polite euphemism for stealing - legitimized by the overpowering strength of the State. Thus it becomes our duty as individuals, and as inhabitants of the earth, to speak out - to make known our views about taxation. Regardless of how much or how little tax we pay, we can say: taxes are wrong.

10 "GOVERNMENT IS NECESSARY FOR INFRASTRUCTURE, POLICE, COURTS."

I am sure we have all heard the statist argument: "Who will build/pay for the roads?"

Roads, sewage, water and electricity and so on are also cited as reasons why a state must exist. How roads could be privately paid for remains such an impenetrable mystery that most people are willing to support the State – and so ensure the eventual and utter destruction of civil society – rather than cede that this problem just might solvable.

So I just want to clarify, would the statist intend to say that without government roads would just stop functioning? That society would never find a voluntary way to coexist and make the infrastructure (that is basically crumbling beneath government currently anyway) work more efficiently? The only way for roads to work is to use violence and coercion on people?

Just because a statist is accustomed to seeing things done by coercive governments taking money from people by force (or threat of force) doesn't mean it's the only way or the right way to do those things. Just because something has been done a certain way since anyone can remember doesn't justify something either. We only just recognized that slavery was wrong last century.

So, *who* would build the roads? That question makes no more sense than asking who will grow the food and who will build the cars and who will operate hardware stores. People will voluntarily create arrangements and companies that suit their own needs. If there's a need for grocery stores, someone will start companies to fill the need. If there's a need for cars, someone will build and sell them. If there's a need for roads, someone will build them and sell the service. The providers and the customers will do all those things because they're in their own interest — not because some coercive, paternalistic government decides for them.

Simply put, government coercion short-circuits the ability of voluntary cooperation to work. In other words, the government you're counting on to fix the problems is getting in the way. They're not only failing to solve the problems, but they are creating the problems.

When I tell people that coercion is wrong and that people have the right to be free and make their own voluntary decisions, they frequently tell me that there are no alternatives. The truth is that voluntary cooperation is a viable alternative, but many people don't want to see it — because it would mean giving up many of the assumptions they have about how society is structured. It would require them to face the reality that the current system is not only immoral, but it's unnecessary.

Freedom *from* Government: Statist Delusions

Voluntaryism is the notion that every person is free to make his own choices about how he interacts with others. If anyone tells you that coercion is necessary, he hasn't looked closely at the evidence. Individual freedom is not only moral, but it's pragmatic.

Government "ownership" of services eliminates competition, and government regulation of private business eliminates competition by forcing individual businesses to merge or fail (unless you are a bank or car manufacturer in some cases) in order to financially survive the regulations. Corporations may prefer to monopolize, but they have to convince people to allow them to do that. Sometimes public opinion disallows this, but government can (and does) coerce people and institutions to accept monopolization, and forces small businesses out of business by adding unsustainable expenditures through taxation and regulation.

Until the US government takes back control of the Federal Reserve central bank, as directed by the constitution the US government, business and citizens will forever be slaves to debt on money that was created out of thin air. The federal income tax on earnings started at the same time as the Federal Reserve Bank, and that is not a coincidence. Worse yet, the Federal Reserve helped start and fund every war the US has been involved in over the last 100 years.

In the perfect market, no consumer or business has excessive power. No one affects price. Every firm is a price-taker for both inputs and outputs. What could be more fair? The perfect market is deemed to embody fair competition. In the beautiful (and non-existent) world of perfect markets, all firms are equal. No one competes "unfairly." Prices are never above long-run costs and profits are driven to zero. There is no waste. Theoretically the economy is in an optimal condition.

Back to the original question ... who will build the roads? And how did the cotton get picked after there were no more slaves?

If we look at the rise of kings, in the early stages of their rise one of the chief advantages of dangerously great and highly centralized authority was that the king would keep "the king's road" open, enabling money and people to get where they wanted to go, by killing those who would set up barricades and shake down travellers.

Lots of roads are privately owned today. The roads in a housing development are often owned by housing association, sometimes voluntary, sometimes compulsory. In some rather small developments, the road is owned by the guy on the top of the hill, who passes around the hat as necessary, but everyone has the right to use the road to access the other properties. Maybe the costs are shared between the owner of one side of such a road, and the owner of another property owns the other side, but everyone has the right to use the road to access any one of five properties. All five properties own an easement on both sides of the road.

In a voluntary society, the small roads would all work like this and the big roads could all be toll roads or community projects funded by local interests. There are many ways to pay for roads, such as electronic or cash tolls, GPS charges, roads maintained by the businesses they lead to, communal organizations and so on.

There is a problem with toll roads though, and with any long linear property. In principle, the owner could make a profit by providing an obstacle rather than access, by charging people to cross his property. This is obviously illegitimate. He can reasonably charge for providing access, for allowing people to drive along his property, but not for allowing people to cross it, charge for providing access to other places, not for blocking access to other places. For a voluntary society to work, people would need to demand a right of access, should be willing to pay for roads, but not pay for road blocks. If people succeed in charging for blocking, rather than providing, access, then trade and commerce would be severely impaired, as it was during the middle ages.

This, illegitimate toll collection, is the greatest problem parts of the world that do not have a central government, for example Somalia, and Afghanistan shortly after the fall of the Taliban. For a voluntary society to succeed economically, most people must believe that they have a right to get to any place they have a right to be. This is already a principle in English common law. An easement over private property is always presumed to exist to allow people to get to any place they have a right to be, but for voluntarism to work, this principle has to be in people's hearts. In an economically successful voluntary society, if you do not want people barging over your property, you have to provide a way around it.

Let us suppose for example someone owns a narrow strip of land running all the way across the country from east to west, perhaps originally acquired to build a road or some such. Now if he makes it into a nice road, it is reasonable that he should be free to charge anyone who wishes to use that road to go from East to West. But what of those who want to go from North to South? Should he be free to make his road into a wall, and charge those who wish to cross it? Obviously not. But how, in a voluntary society would travellers stop him?

In a voluntary society, no one except those affected are going to be concerned to stop him, so there has to be a norm, a widely accepted view, that it is in fact legitimate for people to be free to get from any place they have a right to be, to any other place they have a right to be, and not be stopped, and that if they are unreasonable and obstinately stopped, they can do what it takes to pass, meeting force to force – which implies that if a union, or anyone else, tries to blockade someone, that someone can start shooting. This was in fact the norm, reasonably accepted behavior, in the early years of unionism in the United States, a fact that many people find horrifying, but which seems pretty reasonable to me. The union would set up camp on the key road serving the employer's facility, and sooner or later, the employer would have to start shooting.

This argument takes many forms. You can replace roads with schools, social programs, or any other "service" the government provides. The answer in the cases of both building and paying for services is – whoever needs them. Governments aren't the only force in the world capable of constructing and maintaining roads, and it's not fair to charge everyone when not everyone uses them.

Ask a statist to explain why the state funded tax subsidized (so therefore nominally higher in funding) roads are full of potholes cracks and are constantly in need of repair, but Wal-Mart's privately paved roads and parking lots are smoother than a baby's bottom?

The problem that a water company might build plumbing to a community, and then charge exorbitant fees for supplying it, is equally easy to counter. A truck could deliver bottled water, or the community could invest in a water tower, a competing company could build alternate pipes and so on. None of these problems touch the central rationale for a State. They are *ex post facto* justifications made to avoid the need for critical examination or, heaven forbid, political action. The argument that voluntary free-market monopolies are bad – and that the only way to combat them is to impose compulsory monopolies – is obviously foolish. If voluntary monopolies are bad, then how can coercive monopolies be better?

Due to countless examples of free market solutions to the problem of 'carrier costs', this argument no longer holds the kind of water it used to, so it must be elsewhere that people must turn to justify the continued existence of the State.

In reality the answer to the question of who will provide services is very easy: *We will.*

If we had no state, everyone would likely have vastly more money and resources with which could be used to help anybody, fund any endeavor thought to be a worthy cause and nobody would ever try to stop you. To those who argue that people wouldn't fund some project unless you force them, if you can't get people to voluntarily fund something, then it likely wasn't a worthy cause in the first place.

And no, having a cause collectively deemed worthy does not justify forcibly extracting funds because human lives are not ours to dispose of, and no cause is so great that it deserves to be shielded from public scrutiny.

Trent Goodbaudy

11 "TAKE A BENEFIT FROM THE GOVERNMENT, AND YOU ENDORSE IT."

Who hasn't heard a statist imply or just say outright that if you use what the government provides, then you automatically have to endorse the government.

The answer is simple. What else is there at this point (other than things provided by the government)? People have been letting the government run the country for so long, just about everything has its stamp on it. It's impossible not to benefit (or suffer) from the government's unsolicited meddling in society, but the rub is that it's unsolicited. I never asked the government to do anything. Everything it did, it did on its own, and I claim no responsibility for it, but if it's there and I have a use for it, of course I'm going to take advantage of it. Life takes advantage of its environment. We do not owe the government for forcing us to depend on it.

If you were a slave living on a plantation would you eat the food that your master provided? Would you wear clothes that the master provided? Why would you do that? Would you be supporting slavery by taking a benefit from your master? Or would you feel that after all he has taken from you that is the least he could provide, but absolutely nothing compared to you being free and being able to care for yourself the way you like.

A similar variation on this statement that statists use is that if you use government services you are a hypocrite. This argument would have merit if people were actually voluntarily funding government action despite morally condemning it, but that's just simply not the case at all. The money is forcibly seized from residents. Taxes fund the government "service" and I refuse to use their service by way of moral principle, so does the same in any way discourage the government from providing that service to me? If I am unable to opt-out from taking government benefits can I honestly be called a hypocrite when I am forced to take a "benefit" such as a ticket for not wearing my seatbelt? This all goes back to the use of violence and coercion again. Wouldn't there be an underlying feeling of fear based willingness to submit to the commands of an individual endowed with the ability to use lethal force to insure compliance? In effect they are essentially forcing one to "benefit" from their service and if one does not comply they risk having violence used against them to force compliance in line with the demands of this agent representative of a soul-less corporate entity that doesn't really value me as an individual anyway.

So, just like a slave accepting a meal from his master; just because I have accepted the meal, does not mean that I endorse the masters business practices. Same with accepting a benefit from government; if I need something that the government provides to survive, it cannot be looked at as supporting the system that is oppressing me. In reality I am just making the best of an immoral situation and at least I can have pride in the fact that I am not the aggressor.

On the other side of this argument is the statist that advocates a particular service because they used it and it seemed to be helpful. Unfortunately, personal anecdotes do not suffice as an empirical argument. One person's testimony is not only unverifiable and tainted by bias, but a sample of one experience is far too small to be valid data. Plus this argument is in complete evasion of the moral question of the state. Even if a social service program funded by government took very good care of you, it does not excuse the fact that it is funded by coercion. Being polite about stealing is still stealing. There are plenty of businesses that were helped by the mafia too; does that excuse the mafia's crimes? No. The ends do not justify the means.

Trent Goodbaudy

12 "WHY DON'T YOU GO LIVE SOMEWHERE ELSE, LIKE SOMALIA."

One of the many typical responses statists give to an opponent in a conversation about not supporting the state is, "If you don't like it, leave!" This response has always bothered me. It is such an extreme and insensitive response. It shows no compassion and empathy and proves only how intolerant, cold-hearted and bullying people can be. It's similar to such responses as, "My way or the highway" or in other words, "Act the way I want you to or you can go die by getting run over by cars." It shows no attempt to try to understand the other side and try to reach an arrangement that both sides agree to. It's really just saying, "Well if you don't like it, tough cookie. Go cry to mommy because you won't get any sympathy from me." No moral individual would dare utter such an uncaring, insensitive remark.

What I find interesting though is that statists don't really believe what they are saying. Many statists believe in minimum wage laws for example. If a boss pays their workers a salary which is barely enough to get by, statists demand passing laws forcing employers to pay their workers more. How come they don't say, "Well if you don't like getting paid so little, you can leave and find someone else to pay you more?" What would they think of someone who responded to a poor, desperate person by saying, "Well if you don't like it, you can just leave." Would they think such a person sympathetic to the needs of this poor desperate fellow or a cold-hearted person unwilling to try to understand the desperation that this poor person feels and that maybe it's not so easy just to leave. Many statists believe in passing equal pay laws and laws prohibiting private discrimination. Do they say, "If you don't like getting paid less than men, why don't you just leave or start your own business." What would they think of a person who responded this way? No, the statist doesn't say this. Instead they see what seems like people taking advantage of vulnerable people and people are not in a position of bargaining power equal to others and they try to rectify the situation. What would the typical statist think of someone who said; "Well, I'm not giving up my assault rifles and if you don't like it, well you can just leave and go to another country that bans these kinds of weapons." Would they think of them as a person trying to understand their worries or simply as an unsympathetic bully who couldn't give a rat's behind about other people's needs. Many statists complain about how Wal-Mart is underpaying their workers. What would they say to someone who responded, "If you don't like it leave and find someone to pay you more or if you can't then start your own company (sort of like how the statist will commonly mention to start our own country like it's a piece of cake)." They understand it's not that easy for a person to leave their job (though how they think it's easier to leave an oppressive country, which often involves leaving a job, not to mention one's home and family and friends).

So why don't they have this view consistently? They really truthfully couldn't believe in the "if you don't like it leave" reasoning because when it comes to a cause they believe in they will not be consistent with their previous view. Instead they will put government on a pedestal and continue to allow them to continue taking advantage of people, and sometimes actually even make excuses for government to justify when someone has been harmed by them that under different circumstances they would never approve of themselves.

When a statist compares the United States with whatever country in Africa they're familiar with (and probably couldn't point to on a map), usually they are saying that the country they're talking about is impoverished and/or violent because it is stateless. In this case they are usually completely ignorant about the actual situation in that country, and a quick scan on Wikipedia will make you a veritable expert on that country's politics compared to them. Often, the violence is due to several groups fighting for political control over the country. The poverty is often due to outsiders (like foreign corporations) stealing their resources. Lack of government is not to blame, it's people struggling for power.

The "if you don't like it, you can go live somewhere else" argument isn't really an argument. It's an admission that what you said is true (assuming they said it in response to something that was said to them) and they can't refute it. It's the equivalent of them plugging their ears and singing Ace of Base's 90s hit "The Sign" at the top of their lungs. You can call them out for that, but they won't listen to that either. The conversation is basically over, but you could tell them that you have every right to be here as they do. This land is your land. If they want you off it, they can try to make you. Call them tough guy.

Statists love to support their pet government by arguing that if you don't like it, you're free to leave whenever you want...of course ignoring the fact that you need the government's permission to leave and thus they can stop you if they so desire. But what's really downright evil about this argument is how it's effectively blaming the victim. If a woman complains about how her husband beats her and blows all their money on booze, what would you think of someone who replied by saying it's her fault for staying with him? It really takes a special kind of hate for others to resort to a low blow argument like this and shame on anyone who ever has.

The other statement that a statist will make in support of the government is "at least it's better than living in country 'x'" and mentioned the comparison game in a previous argument, but this one is a bit different. Instead of comparing government to statelessness, they are comparing the government here to the government in a different country to make the one here look better. Just because something is better than something that is worse does not make it right or moral. There's no way to argue with the fact that there are worse governments out there than the United States. It's true, after all. The thing to do is remind the person you're talking to that taking money from people under the threat of violence is always wrong, end of story. Don't let your opponent derail the argument.

13 "WITHOUT RULES, THERE WOULD BE CHAOS."

One of the biggest claims made by a statist is that without rules, there would be chaos. This is a convenient all-purpose statist argument.

This makes about as much sense as the notion that without arranged marriages people would be going around marrying whoever they wanted! It would be definitely be chaos! The correct response to this argument would be "yeah" that's exactly what we want. In case you hadn't noticed, the internet is chaotic fundamentally and that's exactly how we want it. Nature is a tinker not a designer and we owe everything to that fact, the first thing that we need to understand about chaos is that it isn't always bad. Chaos is actually as necessary as order. This is not inherently bad as the argument seems to apply, but if we think deeper about this concept, laws are currently absurdly complex. Nobody can read, remember, or understand them, how in the grace of god are we supposed to comply with all of them?

Politicians can and frequently do disregard their oaths. They even regularly commit outright crimes against their own people with no ill consequence. Most of the time they don't even try to hide it. In reality regulations are up for grabs to the highest bidder, with absolutely no ethics or moral principle basis whatsoever. Many laws that have been legislated also contradict each other. Bankers can scam the public and then get bailouts instead of bankruptcies? And this cycle of destruction and corruption goes on, and on, and on.

Ordinary law and order in a voluntary society is unlikely to be a big problem. One that ordinary people won't think about very much or notice much, except in the sense of large gangs or external governments attempting to become governments.

A statist would like to tell you that without government, everyone would murder, rape, and steal. It wouldn't matter who pays for the roads because they wouldn't be safe!

A proper response to this reckless assertion is "Are you saying the only reason you don't murder, rape and steal is because you're afraid of punishment?" And if that's the case, they are really in no position to be lecturing about morals. Another way to look at this argument is that even if the statist is correct in his assumption that humanity would be not only lawless but also immoral without government, their argument still fails. Because a race of evil humans couldn't be good and moral on their own but they will vote in someone who will force them to? How, in the world does that make anything even close to resembling logical sense?

The only situation where a state could be argued is if most people are evil but only good people get into the government. There is no logical or empirical reason to believe that this is, was or ever will be the situation and I'd really like to know how such a group could remain in power if the rest of the population disagreed with them so passionately.

There is a valid question in this idea however, about how the law would work in a voluntary society without what we think of as a government today. The creation of law from above, or centrally planned law, only became a major part of lawmaking in the English speaking world in the nineteenth century.

In many places and times, law, for example the English Common Law, started with crimes and punishment, and then, from the efforts to ensure that one judge's rulings are consistent with another, lawyers constructed precedent, and then, from precedent, they discovered a legal framework.

Well respected lawyers would examine the decisions of well respected judges, and write books analyzing those decisions, then formulating an account of those decisions in terms of laws that explained their decisions and rendered them consistent with each other. Then if a judge happened to deviate from a law, the lawyer pleading the case could complain, and did complain, that the judge violated precedent.

If the common law of England was actually written down anywhere as words on paper, it was written down in Blackstone's "Commentaries on the Laws of England" — but the laws he was commenting on were for the most part not documents issued by judges or legislators but interpretations of the conduct of judges whose conduct was widely accepted as right and just, much as Newton's laws are interpretations of the behavior of moving objects.

In a voluntary society, the nearest thing to legislation would be when one group of people made a compromise with another, to agree on rules covering conflicts between them.

The argument that you need law to be decreed from above, centrally planned law, is a silly argument, no different from the argument that you need the state to issue paper money, etc. The state does lots of stuff today, that it has not always done in the past, and one of the things it did not always do in the past was legislate.

Today the state does "insert service", therefore we cannot have voluntarism, for in voluntarism no one would do "insert service". This argument stems from ignorance. In a voluntary society, the only way we can have law, or consistent rules between people protected by one defense agency, and people protected by another is for one agency to impose its rules on the other by either force or negotiation.

In a voluntary society; public good laws would be under provided, and private good laws would be adequately provided.

A private good law is a law where it is in the interests of a particular person to have the law enforced against a particular offender, for example the laws against robbery, rape and so forth. A public good law is a law where it is arguably in everyone's interest that it be enforced in general, but it is not in the particular interest of any particular person that it be enforced against any other particular person.

Most private good laws are uncontroversial, universally accepted, and almost universally enforced. Public good laws tend to be somewhat controversial, selectively enforced, and far from universally accepted, and the many infamous governmental crimes, for example the Jim Crow laws, were enforcement of public good laws. Laws prohibiting racism are also public good laws as much as laws commanding racism, but prohibiting racism tends to have effects curiously similar to commanding it.

One example of a fairly uncontroversial public good law is the law requiring cars to limit their pollution. A particularly offensive car would offend particular people enough for them to harass the owner, but many mildly polluting cars would not, even if their combined effect was intolerable. So in a voluntary society, cars might well be more polluting than they are at present. On the other hand, rivers and the like would be owned by particular small groups of people, who would likely be willing to defend their condition, whereas governments have been notoriously unwilling to protect a river against a concentrated interest, so rivers would probably be less polluted. Most communist countries had far more severe levels of pollution than most capitalist countries, because it was not in the interests of any particular person to defend any particular property against any particular pollution. Even when the state is present, private good laws tend to be enforced, and public good laws not enforced, thus the absence of the state is unlikely to make as large a difference in practice as it does in theory.

If a crime has a specific identifiable victim, who is the victim of a specific identifiable act, then that law is a private good, because each particular individual will have reason to enter into arrangements to ensure that such crimes are punished or avenged when committed against himself.

In order to suppress drugs, or exterminate Arabs, you have to appeal to people's altruism and self-sacrifice. People are very willing to be altruistic when they are voting, because they are mostly voting someone else's money. They are a lot more selfish when they are paying with their own money.

I would be willing to do what is necessary to obtain a defense contract that says that if I am robbed or murdered, I will be avenged. I will not be willing to do the same for a defense contract that says some stranger far away will be avenged, still less a defense contract that says some stranger far away will be punished for taking unapproved drugs.

In a voluntary society, private goods get supplied because it is in the interest of particular people or small groups to supply them. For example there is usually someone who wants particular vengeance against a particular mugger. Public goods are under supplied, because although it might supposedly be in the interests of "everyone" that they be supplied it is not in the interest of any particular person or small group that they be supplied.

The under supply of public goods is often argued as a defect of voluntarism, but during the twentieth century, the most important public goods provided were aggressive war, genocide, artificial famine, and mass murder, so if we lack those, I will not much miss the others.

Even if ninety percent of the population support a public good law, it will not be effectually enforced because it will not be in the interest of any one person to enforce it, but if a substantial minority support a private good law, it will be enforced, because it is in the interest of each particular person to enforce it as it affects himself.

A public good is something that is supposedly good for everyone, perhaps really is good for everyone, but does not directly benefit particular individuals, so there is no one individual who has a direct personal interest in doing something about this public good in any one particular case. A private good is something where in each particular case much of the benefit goes to a particular person or quite small group, so that in each particular case there is a particular person or small group who has good reason to make this good thing happen, good reason to themselves bear the costs of making this good thing happen.

If someone buys or snorts cocaine, there is no pissed off victim, there is no one pushing hard to make enforcement happen in any one particular case, so enforcement against liquor or cocaine generally would not happen, and so in an voluntary society such laws, by custom and precedent, would cease to be socially acceptable grounds for the use of force against someone, and thus cease to be laws.

Those offenses that would make any man use force in response will be illegal. Those offenses that would not make most people use force in response will be legal.

Collecting money and manpower to enforce a law against burglary would be like selling insurance. "If you contribute, you can put a sticker on your house that says protected by XYZ". Collecting money and manpower to enforce a law against prostitution or abortion would be like collecting money for charity or manpower for a neighborhood cleanup. It could be done, it often would be done, and the willingness to engage in violent confrontation, the willingness to hurt, upset, and anger people, would be vastly less.

The average person is willing to bring out his gun and look for trouble if his next door neighbor is being burgled. A similar enthusiasm for trouble about a dirty book store seems unlikely, because the dirty book shop does not threaten any particular individual the way a burglar next door threatens someone. If you are a long way from the dirty bookstore, you probably do not care very much. If you are right next door to the dirty bookstore, then you still do not care the way you care about robbery, murder, and rape, and in addition the proprietor and some of the regular customers are real people to you, and you would not want to make them unhappy.

Burglary would likely be illegal in voluntary society, and dirty bookstores would likely be legal, because lots of people are willing to shoot burglars, whereas only a dangerous nut would be willing to shoot a proprietor of a dirty book store.

A person who attacks the owner of a dirty book store might attack me. A person who sells dirty books is unlikely to attack me. Thus I would be motivated to support the use of force against someone who used force against the proprietor of a dirty bookstore, and would not be motivated to use force or support the use of force against someone selling dirty books.

That use of force that most ordinary peaceable individuals are inclined to employ will be legal, and thus the activities they use it against illegal. That use of force that only weird, scary, dangerous, aggressive people are inclined to employ will be illegal.

The age of consent would become a matter of parental discretion, which does not much resemble today's written law, but does resemble today's practice.

If there were important issues of law where the answer was unclear, and also large numbers of people were likely to care passionately about these issues and be willing to kill and die over issues, then voluntary law would not converge. I do not see this. All issues of law that are genuinely open to question are either obscure and complex things that most people are unlikely to get very excited about, or even comprehend, or they are public good laws that just will not get enforced very effectively anyway.

All in all we would be immensely better off living under the non-aggression principle in a voluntary society. People who say that there would be chaos without order are really just repeating a mantra. Who decides what the rules are? What if a rule is unfair or just wrong? What recourse do people have when the right thing to do is against the rules? You don't have to accept someone else's authority just because you're told to. Freedom means being able to decide our own rules. We're a social species. Most of us want to cooperate most of the time, and the number of uncooperative people will not change in the absence of big brother.

Trent Goodbaudy

CONCLUSION

In conclusion, I would like to discuss the final delusion that a statist will ambush you with typically just before they change the subject or emotionally overreact. They will usually say "Why don't you name an example of a community that has ever run itself successfully without government? It's never been done before!"

If you want to really frustrate statists who resort to this argument, just ask them "Can you name me one society in history who kept their government small and unobtrusive? Has there ever even been a government that didn't overstep its authority, grow uncontrollably, and eventually collapse as surely as the tides go out?"

When they stand there with a blank look in their eyes, you'll know how much they actually care about empiricism and historical precedence...

The truth is, examples are all around you. The vast majority of your everyday life is self-governed and you would never have it any other way. Spontaneous order and the excellence that comes from voluntary trade is everywhere if you bother to look.

It just so also happens that every other living species on the planet seems to run itself successfully without government intervention just fine. Elephants, zebras, peacocks, chickens, spiders, dolphins, pigs, eagles, bats, and tufted puffins (a real bird that lives on the Oregon coast) are just a few of the millions of examples of societies on earth that have gotten along just fine without a central government. The human race is another. We invented government, which means we were around before it existed. The question is: Did we invent government in order to solve problems? The answer to that question might require a degree in anthropology, but we can take a shortcut and look at the present. Does government solve problems now? Is our nation an example of a successfully run society? Rules were created, and every one of them is broken all the time. They're broken too often for most of the rule breakers to be punished. Nobody even knows what all the rules are because each one is a thousand-plus page document that is voted on based on a petty system of bribery and counter-bribery played out in the legislature. Our economy is doomed to collapse because it is a giant pyramid scheme dreamed up by the government not all that long ago. Rules do not solve problems. They only define people as criminals.

Yes it is true, that no society has ever dismantled their government without an intention of creating a new one but that's beside the point. A stateless society is an entirely new idea and one that has worked in every small way it has been tried. There is no reason to doubt that it can't work on a larger scale and to claim that you know beyond any shadow of a doubt that it can't is simply irrational fear of change talking. Let it go, it's not healthy.

Freedom *from* Government: Statist Delusions

We *do* need to at least decentralize the perceived "power" inherent in government. Milgram and the Stanford Prison experiments proved beyond doubt that power is always abused. Privatized civic services would be just like any other business, but run for the good of the people. Do a bad job? You're fired. We don't have to wait until the next "election" cycle and be constantly bombarded by lies and propaganda.

The fact that this choice is becoming easy to identify does not mean the right alternative will be easy to implement. Convincing skeptics of the long-neglected case for freedom and personal responsibility is not going to happen right away — you can't cede your leading institutions to statists for decades and expect to turn things around overnight. But the second alternative, the one that is so easy — and obviously for some, so tempting — is surrender and allow the violence, coercion, and abuses of power to continue and the steep decline of personal freedom and likely much more than that. Accommodation only works in a normal order where both sides have the same core moral values but differ on how to validate them. It does not work when one side is looking to defeat the other.

While people were dumpster diving in New York City after Hurricane Sandy, voters were telling exit-pollsters that they were pleased with Obama's response to the disaster. But all he really did was show up for a photo-op and looked presidential and bipartisan. Forget the people freezing and starving because the bloated government couldn't get there fast enough to help anyone, as long as it looked like someone cared they were cool with it. Even in places like Greece, rather than facing reality the people there are rioting in the streets. I would like to think that we are on the verge of a new age of enlightenment, where we can experience a life where violence is obsolete, with the driving emotion being love and not fear.

Contrary to the views of many, enlightenment is not about bliss. Enlightenment is not about happiness; it is about the truth coming in and destroying the lie. It does not elate you like a drug, it is more like someone turning on the lights, and now you can see all the filth and feces smeared on the walls. The truth has been hidden, obfuscated, twisted, and spun; people operate on irrational systems without ever questioning them. If you can manipulate a language, and how its words are defined you can manipulate thinking. This confusion is being used against us, and if we allow it to continue, we deserve what is coming.

ANOTHER MUST READ BY
TRENT GOODBAUDY

FREEDOM from GOVERNMENT; HOW TO RECLAIM YOUR POWER

WWW.FREEDOM*from*GOVERNMENT.ORG

This is your handbook for dealing with government on your terms. Learn how to beat any victimless charges, what to say to law enforcement, the problem with attorneys (and why you NEVER want to hire one), why statute and legislation only apply to you if you allow it, the difference between a "right" and a privilege, what it means to be truly free and responsible for yourself and your estate, the history of our legal system (and why it is so messed up), how to get remedy for
inherent rights violations, and everything else you will
NEED TO MAKE THEM LEAVE YOU ALONE FOREVER!

AVAILABLE NOW AT
SHOP.TRENTGOODBAUDY.COM
AND AMAZON.COM

Trent Goodbaudy

Freedom *from* Government: Statist Delusions

ALSO BY TRENT GOODBAUDY

YOU DON'T WANT TO READ WHAT THIS MAN HAS TO SAY!

WWW.YOUDONTWANT.COM

Imagine if you could know the answers to just the important things about this life, would you spend years searching for them?

Trent's philosophy about life is unparalleled, and his views are unconventional. If your audience is looking for answers to life's toughest questions, Trent has done an excellent job of answering them and at the same time provides real, sensible advice for improving other aspects of life as well.

THE REBIRTH OF MANKIND HOMO EVOLUTIS

WWW.EVOLUTISBOOK.COM

While we were recovering from the tragedy of September 11, 2001 the global powers that be were making plans for humanity that were so large and so sweeping, they needed to keep the general public in the dark about what they were planning.

With the rapid advancement of new technology such as genetics, nanotechnology, artificial intelligence, synthetic biology, and electronics we will be able to augment and change our very bodies at the molecular level. The convergence of these technologies spell out some exciting prospects for the future, but at the same time there exists a danger so great that extinction of every living organism on the planet is closer than we think. We must be aware of our past, to know where the future leads, and we must not remain apathetic. Ignorance is not bliss... it is terminal.
Awareness is the cure.

These titles available now at shop.TrentGoodbaudy.com and amazon.com in both paperback and kindle editions

Trent Goodbaudy

ABOUT THE AUTHOR

Trent Goodbaudy currently lives in Hillsboro, Oregon and is a professional writer, blogger, activist, photographer and web developer. Trent has a background in Aviation Maintenance Technology, Computer Science, Computer Information Systems, Programming, Design, Administrative Law, Spirituality, the true history of our planet and eventually the secrets of the Universe.

Trent is driven to write his books out of a passion for helping others, and he believes that awareness and knowing exactly who you are, and who you are not is the most empowering concept one can learn in life.